·

American Justice 2016

Also by Lincoln Caplan

*Up Against the Law: Affirmative
Action and the Supreme Court*

*Skadden: Power, Money, and the
Rise of a Legal Empire*

An Open Adoption

*The Tenth Justice: The Solicitor General
and the Rule of Law*

*The Insanity Defense and the
Trial of John W. Hinckley, Jr*

American Justice 2016

The Political Supreme Court

Lincoln Caplan

PENN

UNIVERSITY OF PENNSYLVANIA PRESS

PHILADELPHIA

Published by
University of Pennsylvania Press
Philadelphia, Pennsylvania 19104-4112
www.upenn.edu/pennpress

Garrett Epps, Consulting Editor

Printed in the United States of America

A Cataloging-in-Publication record is available from the Library of Congress.

Cover design by John Hubbard

ISBN 978-0-8122-4890-6 (hardcover)
ISBN 978-0-8122-9372-2 (e-book)

For Rob Shapiro

Contents

Introduction

Justice Ruth Bader Ginsburg gave the Supreme Court a brief but colossal jolt soon after the end of the 2015 term, when she denounced the fury-fueled candidacy of Donald Trump to be president of the United States. She called him a "faker" in interviews with prominent outlets in journalism and declared, "I can't imagine what this place would be—I can't imagine what the country would be—with Donald Trump as our President. For the country, it could be four years. For the Court, it could be—I don't even want to contemplate that."

Trump retorted, "I think it's highly inappropriate that a United States Supreme Court judge gets involved in a political campaign, frankly. I think it's a disgrace to the Court, and I think she should apologize to the Court. I couldn't believe it when I saw it." He accompanied that, predictably, with a tweet: "Justice Ginsburg of the U.S. Supreme Court has embarrassed all by making very dumb political statements about me. Her mind is shot—resign!"

The disapproval from the liberal, Democrat-appointed Ginsburg was mild compared to what leading conservative Republicans had been saying. They called him, among other things, "a race-baiting, xenophobic religious bigot"; "a dishonest demagogue who plays to our worst fears"; and "a madman." For a moment, Ginsburg's comments seemed to do no more than confirm the exceedingly abnormal nature of the 2016 election, especially of Trump's campaign.

He was carrying the Republican banner, but he was a kind of performance artist, not a politician—a self-appointed celebrity who had morphed into a tycoon as a result of being a celebrity and who was trying to pull off the same trick in politics to become the leader of the free world. Ginsburg might have thought she had a license to call him out because she had acquired some fame, too. As "Notorious RBG," she was celebrated as a heroine, brilliant and brave, for standing up to the Court's conservative majority.

Even among admirers of hers, however, the moment gave way to harsh judgment. The Code of Conduct for United States Judges states that "A Judge Should Refrain from Political Activity." Under "General Prohibitions," it spells out that a judge should not "make speeches for a political organization or candidate, or publicly endorse or oppose a candidate for public office."

The code does not bind the justices, so in the strictest sense, she did not disobey it. But Chief Justice John G. Roberts Jr. had pushed back against serious congressional pressure that the justices vote to make it binding on members of the Court, by saying that it was unnecessary because all of them already followed it. Clearly, Ginsburg did not when she sounded off.

According to the code, her public opposition to Trump as a candidate was plainly unethical. It was almost certainly grounds for a request that she recuse herself from any case reaching the Court that, like *Bush v. Gore* in 2000, would decide the presidency. It was arguably grounds for her recusal if Trump became president, in any Court case that would directly affect his authority.

But that was not what made Ginsburg's gaffe so unsettling. In the *Los Angeles Times*, the paper's longtime

Supreme Court correspondent David G. Savage wrote that her "comments dealt a clear setback to Chief Justice John G. Roberts Jr. and his effort to keep the court separate from the poisonous partisan politics of Washington." In fact, her comments were a reminder that the Court is not separate from politics. They were unnerving, even after she apologized for them, because they raised the question of how her views on politics had influenced her votes in Court cases and how they would in the future.

The Supreme Court is a political institution. Saying that is like saying there is a global economy: both are simply facts. Some parts of this reality should not be controversial. As a body that the US Constitution requires ("The judicial Power of the United States, shall be vested in one supreme Court, and in such inferior Courts as the Congress may from time to time ordain and establish."), the Court is a product of politics—of the convention that created that document and of its ratification by the states. The justices are products of politics—the nominees of presidents elected by a majority of the electoral college, appointed with the consent of a majority of senators elected by their states.

Other parts of the reality are sometimes controversial. The Supreme Court's decisions are final, neither reviewed by nor subject to approval of another tribunal, so the Court operates differently from any other court in the United States. It usually follows its own precedents when deciding cases, but it is not bound by them the way the lower federal courts and state courts are. It has the power to put aside or overturn its own precedents, and it does. In cases where no principle of law leads to a result that all or most of the justices agree on, they draw on their views about policy—politics in its functional form.

This is the most controversial way the Court is political. The Supreme Court makes or creates law in almost all its cases, when it is interpreting a hard-to-understand portion of a federal statute and especially when it is applying a clause of the Constitution to facts its shapers could not have contemplated more than two centuries ago. In making those interpretations or applications, the justices sometimes draw on more than their legal acumen or judicial philosophy.

They draw on their prior legal experiences, whether as a prosecutor, a federal policy-maker, a scholar, or a judge; on their outlooks shaped by the family, culture, and region of the country they grew up in; and on their religious and other values, including their political ones. This politics is not always partisan: in the recent past, for example, Justices Harry A. Blackmun and John Paul Stevens, who were appointed by Republican presidents, drifted to the left during their time on the Court and, at the end of their long tenures, regularly voted for liberal outcomes. But this politics, often called ideology, involves a distinct view about how the Court should allocate basic elements of society: power, opportunity, duty, responsibility, and many others.

The ideal for the Court has long been that it should make decisions about law without regard to politics. The rule of law—the idea that government, and not particular men or women, is empowered and constrained by law—depends on this ideal of separation. For that reason, the Constitution gives the justices life tenure, as long as they maintain "good behaviour," and guarantees that their compensation "shall not be diminished during their continuance in office." They have life tenure so they will decide cases impartially, including independently of politics. They cannot be punished for their judicial decisions by having their pay cut or getting fired.

This ideal serves valuable purposes. When the Court rules in a contentious case, faith in the rule of law raises the chances that even the losers in the case will accept it and not react in protest. Al Gore's decision to abide by the Court decision in 2000 that made George W. Bush president is a prime example. When American institutions are functioning poorly, and a consequence is the ill treatment of a racial, ethnic, religious, or other minority group, the existence of the Court—with its duty to apply the Constitution fairly on behalf of all Americans—can be a source of hope.

But the ideal that the Court makes decisions about law without regard to politics has never been a reality. The Constitution makes explicit the basic link between law and politics through the government it established. The legislative and executive branches are called the political branches because voters elect members of Congress to serve in the first branch and the president and vice-president to lead the second. Congress makes federal law through statutes, and the executive branch carries out much of that law through enforcement and rulemaking. The federal judiciary as a whole, not just the Supreme Court, makes law by interpreting the Constitution and other federal law, and the judiciary sometimes shapes policy. Those rulings are, in a basic sense, political, especially when the Court is fulfilling its role in the American constitutional system in dealing with another branch.

The basic structure of the federal government—three distinct branches with separated yet coordinated powers and the duty to use them to check and balance one another—is a structure of law designed to discipline the excesses of politics. Law is the system of rules devised to regulate society. Politics is the means for distributing and exercising power through government institutions, political parties, interest groups, and so on. The courts are among the government institutions. In interpreting and applying rules, law enacts policies about governance, which are products of debate among competing interests carried out through politics. American law and politics are indistinguishable at the most fundamental level.

When Ginsburg said, "I can't imagine what this place would be—I can't imagine what the country would be—with Donald Trump as our president," she was referring to the Supreme Court ("this place") and the real possibility that the next president would have the chance to appoint four justices. She was then eighty-three, Justice Anthony M. Kennedy was almost eighty, Justice Stephen G. Breyer was almost seventy-eight, and there was already a vacancy resulting from the death, in February of 2016, of Justice Antonin G. Scalia at seventy-nine. Politics loomed large over the Court.

Immediately after Scalia's death, there was virtually instant agreement between the right and the left that the replacement for Scalia would likely determine whether, in the near term, the Court continued to be generally conservative or became more liberal: the remaining justices split evenly between four conservative justices and four liberal ones. The Senate majority leader Mitch McConnell, the conservative Republican from Kentucky, and the Senate judiciary committee chairman Charles Grassley, the conservative Republican from Iowa, announced that the 2016 presidential election, as of February more than eight months away, should decide who selected Scalia's replacement.

Their rationale was that in an election year, the voters should have a voice in deciding who replaces Scalia through their selection of the next president, because the choice was fundamentally political. Their premise was that the Senate had the power to transfer to an unelected successor the authority of the current president to nominate a justice. The Republicans were exercising their political power as the majority party in the Senate—they took it back in 2014 for the first time in a decade—by refusing to consider Obama's nominee even before the president named one. There was no way to stop them under the Constitution.

John Roberts famously testified at his 2005 confirmation hearing to be chief justice that if approved, he would serve as an umpire who called balls and strikes. He would apply or interpret law rather than make it. The full quotation went,

> Judges are not politicians who can promise to do certain things in exchange for votes. I have no agenda, but I do have a commitment. If I am confirmed, I will confront every case with an open mind. I will fully and fairly analyze the legal arguments that are presented. I will be open to the considered views of my colleagues on the bench. And I will decide every case based on the record, according to the rule of law, without fear or favor, to the best of my ability. And I will remember that it's my job to call balls and strikes and not to pitch or bat.

When he portrayed a justice as an umpire, Roberts stirred wide skepticism about whether he would keep his promise of minimizing the scope and power of the job as it has long been done. By the beginning of the 2015 term, though, his observation about judges not being politicians was the more relevant. The record of the Roberts Court made clear that his way of framing the problem did not fit current reality. It was not that justices gained their seats on the Court by promising to vote in specific ways: they did not need to make that promise. A president's team did not need to extract it because the future justices' votes in general were generally predictable.

During the previous five terms, for the first time in American history, the Court issued the majority of its ideological 5–4 rulings along party lines. The five conservative justices, appointed by Republicans, were Roberts and Justices Kennedy, Scalia, Clarence Thomas, and Samuel A. Alito Jr. They regularly made up the majority. The four liberals, appointed by Democrats, were Justices Ginsburg, Breyer, Sonia Sotomayor, and Elena Kagan. They were regularly in dissent.

Decisions along these lines—favoring the interests of corporations over those of individuals, gutting the power of labor unions, making it more difficult for individuals to bring civil rights claims against government officials and agencies as well as corporate officers and corporations, striking down the heart of the Voting Rights Act, and so on—reflected the view of political scientists that, by some measures, the Roberts Court during his first decade as chief was the most conservative in more than half a century and likely the most conservative since the 1930s.

Roberts could not keep the Court separate from the politics of Washington, because as a political institution, the Court had always been bound up with politics. He could not keep the Court separate from partisan politics because it had made prominent and divisive decisions throughout his time as chief justice that contributed to the partisanship. By the time of Scalia's death in the middle of the 2015 term, politics seemed to define the Court by determining who would pick his successor and what the Court's new political inclination would be. Yet the overarching challenge in understanding the Court as a political institution is recognizing how it remains a Court. Justices draw on their political and other values in making decisions about cases, but they do so while making judgments about law, and law constrains those judgments.

Sometimes, a justice goes along with a majority of the Court not because he or she agrees with everything the majority opinion says but for strategic reasons—to avoid a 5–4 split likely to be seen as partisan, for example. But that kind of strategic choice does not mean the justices are cavalier about their role.

The politicization of the Court is often presented as either-or: if the Court retreated from politics, the thought goes, it would act properly by making legal decisions. But it is both a political institution and a legal one, and it should be understood as being both.

The first Supreme Court argument I covered was in *United States v. Nixon* in 1974, the case establishing the principle that the Court has the last word in defining the reach of presidential power. I was a summer intern at *The New Republic* magazine in Washington, DC, between my first and second years of law school. The Burger Court unanimously declared that the president is not "above the law" and rejected the claim by Richard M. Nixon that his position as president gave him the privilege of refusing to turn over tape recordings about the Watergate scandal made in the Oval Office. He resigned soon after in disgrace.

I have since covered the Court for *The New Yorker* and as a member of the editorial board of the *New York Times*, attending arguments there regularly from 1985 to 1987 and from 2010 to 2013 and otherwise following and writing about the Court on and off for forty-plus years while writing more broadly about legal affairs. I have not been a perennial Court correspondent, but I have reported there enough to know the challenges of the task.

I am attracted to something called the legal-process school. During the 1940s and '50s, among leading legal scholars, the school was the most influential way of thinking about the American constitutional system. Today, the primary question about a Supreme Court case is: what is the right outcome in substantive law? Rather than focusing on outcomes, the legal-process school showed how "process"—rules of procedure but also different parts of federal and state government that affect the way a dispute is resolved—shaped substantive law.

The school focused on institutional competence, asking which institution should make a legal decision and how: The federal or a state government? An executive agency, the legislature, or a court? A trial court or a court of appeals? If a trial court, a judge or a jury?

The premise of the school was that the essential function of the Supreme Court and of federal courts in general was to resolve disputes that were properly before them and to leave policy-making to the states and the other federal branches, except when policy was inextricably tied to law. It viewed American law and government as an elaborate, judicious, and progressive system and provided an authoritative map.

The school encouraged skepticism about the Supreme Court's assertion of its power. That has proved useful for me during the decades I have written about the Court. Throughout this period, it has increasingly asserted its power while growing increasingly conservative, led by conservative chief justices appointed by Republicans since 1969.

The political scientist Lee Epstein, who is a leader among scholars doing empirical studies of the institution, called it "The Republican Court," which, at the end of the 2015 term, completed its forty-seventh year. That span is strikingly significant: one-fifth of the Court's history and three-fifths of its modern era (commonly said to begin in 1937, as I discuss in chapter 2).

This book is called *American Justice 2016* as the third in an annual series the University of Pennsylvania Press inaugurated with *American Justice 2014: Nine Clashing Visions on the Supreme Court* by Garrett Epps. In the series, the Press asks a journalist who covers the Court to write a thematic account of the current Court term, with the proviso that the book be completed within the month after the Court hands down its last ruling.

For that reason, this book is a hybrid: written at the pace of journalism, yet with the aim of providing the perspective of a monograph. Because of the tight schedule, there was little time to put the book aside and come back to it with fresh eyes, add examples where they are needed, clarify steps of argument, and so forth. This is, as the cliché goes, a first rough draft of history about a term when history mattered.

The term was perhaps the best one in almost a half century for focusing on the Court as a political institution. It provided an unusual opportunity to understand how the Court's character as a political institution affects the law it makes and why some changes taking account of this reality would benefit the Court and the country—in how justices are chosen, in how long they serve, and in how journalism covers their decisions, among others.

The term was also a good one for reminders that, while a political institution, it remains a legal one at the pinnacle of the American constitutional system. When the Court is functioning properly, it tempers politics into effective law or concentrates solely on law.

When it is not, it allows politics to cloud and contaminate law and reinforce its political side, which in recent decades has sometimes led the Court to act as if it is supreme in that system. The 2015 term made clear that it is not.

The Immigration Case

Why did the states that challenged Barack Obama's 2014 executive order about immigration file their lawsuit in Brownsville, Texas? Why did they choose that small, poor, and outlying city on the American border with Mexico as the place to challenge the president's authority under a longtime statute to make a big change in national immigration law?

Andrew S. Hanen was then the only active federal district judge in the Brownsville Division of the Southern District of Texas, so it was very likely that he would hear the case. Lawyers for the states clearly wanted that to happen. In the large bloc of states with Republican governors that brought the lawsuit, Texas was the lead plaintiff. Greg Abbott, the Republican who was then attorney general of Texas and who became the state's governor, led the lawyers for the group.

They had forum-shopped, as lawyers sometimes do, apparently to have the case heard by the federal judge in the United States whom they considered most likely to provide a favorable ruling. They got the judge they wanted. The US Court of Appeals for the Fifth Circuit, which includes Louisiana, Mississippi, and Texas and is headquartered in New Orleans, would hear any appeal in the case. It is the most conservative circuit in the country. For this case, depending on the appeals-court judges assigned to hear any appeal, it was likely to be the most favorable.

At sixty-one, Hanen had been on the federal bench since President George W. Bush appointed him in 2002. For the most part, he had shown himself to be competent and cautious and averse to controversy and risk, sometimes taking months to decide immigration matters that lawyers thought he could have resolved quickly. Occasionally, on the bench, said a lawyer who appeared before him regularly, his face seemed to express the anguish he was inflicting on himself—how uncomfortable he felt about a situation he could have rectified easily yet chose not to.

He also had a major blind spot, the lawyer said. After presiding over many cases involving Mexican drug smugglers, he gave the impression of viewing them as typical: he seemed to regard all Mexican and other Latino immigrants as similarly disreputable. That bias explained best his intemperate criticism of Obama's immigration policies, which he included in judicial opinions, in language more often used to complain about politics than to reason about law.

In 2013, he presided over a case about the smuggling of a ten-year-old girl from El Salvador to Virginia, which resulted in the conviction of the woman who had transported her. The girl's mother, in the United States illegally, had paid the transporter six thousand dollars in advance. A Supreme Court ruling and a federal statute reinforcing the ruling's terms required the government to reunite the girl and her mother, regardless of her immigration status, which it did.

In a judicial opinion about the case, Hanen wrote that, in carrying out this policy, the government had completed "the criminal mission of individuals who are violating the border security of the United States" in "a dangerous course of action." He wrote that drug "cartels control the entire smuggling process," so, in completing this operation, the government was colluding with the cartels by "helping fund these evil ventures." He concluded, "The D.H.S."—Department of Homeland Security—"should cease telling the citizens of the United States that it is enforcing our border security laws because it clearly is not."

The US Justice Department did not ask the judge to recuse himself from the 2014 case, so that one of the sixty or so other federal district judges in Texas would handle the case. It rarely seeks recusal of a judge. When it does, the request is considered so weighty that the US attorney general must approve it. In this instance, Hanen's comments about the government's collusion with drug cartels in evil ventures and its failure to enforce America's border security laws likely did not rise to the level of bias that would have required his recusal.

The first criterion was that those comments had to be based on a source of information outside the case. In this instance, they were arguably based on the case's evidence. The second was that they had to "reveal such a high degree of favoritism or antagonism as to make fair judgment impossible," as Justice Antonin Scalia defined the standard for recusal in a Supreme Court opinion. Hanen's comments were frankly disapproving of some government actions, but they arguably did not reach that level of hostility. Still, Hanen's comments added to the signs that this obviously political case was before a judge likely inclined to agree with the side that brought it.

Texas and eventually twenty-five other red states brought the case called *Texas v. the United States.* No blue states joined them. It was among the thirty-one lawsuits against the US government that Texas brought while Abbott was the attorney general, as the *Texas Tribune* reported, "a point of pride for the state's Republican leaders." The lawsuit had a political purpose, it was politically constructed, and it became the most political case of the Supreme Court's 2015 term. It showed how politics attacked, infiltrated, and became the law, to the discredit of the judiciary and the Court.

In the legal complaint, the plaintiffs contended: "This lawsuit is not about immigration. It is about the rule of law, presidential power, and the structural limits of the U.S. Constitution." Much of the rest of the complaint contradicted the first sentence while harping on the second. It had the tone of a deeply political document. It was also tactically political: as an example of America's dangerous immigration policies, the complaint included a mention of the one that supposedly "encouraged international child smuggling across the Texas-Mexico border," as the 2013 Hanen opinion had asserted.

The case was about a new immigration program called Deferred Action for Parents of Americans and Lawful Permanent Residents, or DAPA. Deferred action was shorthand for a decision by the Department of Homeland Security to exercise its discretion in how it enforced the law by deferring the deportation of someone in the United States illegally. Announced in November of 2014, the program went as far as Obama and his Justice Department believed that the president had the discretion to go, under current federal immigration statutes, to change immigration priorities. Obama took this step after conservative Republicans in Congress blocked the House of Representatives from voting on a bipartisan and comprehensive immigration reform bill in 2013, which the Senate had passed by sixty-eight to thirty-two.

Here is how Obama announced the program: "My fellow Americans, tonight, I'd like to talk with you about immigration. For more than 200 years, our tradition of welcoming immigrants from around the world has given us a tremendous advantage over other nations. It's kept us youthful, dynamic, and entrepreneurial. It has shaped our character as a people with limitless possibilities—people not trapped by our past, but able to remake ourselves as we choose. But today, our immigration system is broken—and everybody knows it."

Some immigrants played by the rules, he said, while others flouted them. Business owners who offered good wages and benefits faced competition that paid less to undocumented immigrants. But undocumented immigrants who wanted to become responsible Americans could not, so they remained in the shadows. It had been this way for decades, and America had done little about that.

The bill that Obama had worked on with Congress would have doubled the number of border patrol agents while giving undocumented immigrants a pathway to citizenship if they paid a fine, started paying their taxes, and went to the back of the line. The best way to solve this problem would have been to pass that kind of law, but since that had not happened, he had the legal authority as president to take the same kinds of actions that previous Democratic and Republican presidents took to help make the immigration system fairer and more just.

John Boehner, the Republican from Ohio who at the time was Speaker of the House of Representatives and a leader of the opposition, responded to President Obama like this: "The American people want both parties to focus on solving problems together; they don't support unilateral action from a president who is more interested in partisan politics than working with the people's elected representatives. That is not how American democracy works."

Obama had said he was "not a king" and "not the emperor" and that he was "bound by the Constitution," Boehner went on, but now he was contradicting himself. By ignoring the will of the American people, he had "cemented his legacy of lawlessness and squandered what little credibility he had left." Republicans were left with the responsibility of upholding their oath of office. "We will not shrink from this duty, because our allegiance lies with the American people," Boehner said. "We will listen to them, work with our members, and protect the Constitution."

In a dozen years, as a result of the fear of foreigners triggered by the terrorist attacks in September of 2001 and of polarization in American politics so strong that it became an arena for accusation and acrimony rather than for doing the business of democracy, immigration had been turned upside down. It went from being an area of policy that leaders of both parties insisted must be fixed with wide-ranging, bipartisan reform to the country's most disruptive and troubling political issue.

Many on the left favored a new law that would provide a path to citizenship for law-abiding and productive immigrants in the United States illegally, but it was a limited segment of the left with a stake in the issue. Some on the right agreed with that goal. Others said the path must be punitive enough to discourage people from coming here illegally. Others still—nativists—opposed immigration reform altogether: basically, they said that immigrants from Mexico and other Hispanic countries were making the United States less American. At its core, the disagreement was about whether the United States should be an open society, with prudent policies to protect it from dangerous would-be immigrants, or whether it should become a closed one.

Under Obama's proposed program, immigrants could apply to stay in the United States for three years and, in addition, could apply to work legally in the country if they had been in the United States since January of 2010 or before and if they had children who were American citizens or lawful permanent residents. The program was intended to hold undocumented immigrants accountable yet to benefit those who merited the support: it sought to get them to register and pass "criminal and national security background checks" and to pay "their fair share of taxes"; it would let parents who passed those checks stay in the United States for a limited amount of time "without fear of deportation."

This deferral of deportation was the third of "three critical elements" in the program. The first was "cracking down on illegal immigration at the Mexican border" to increase the likelihood that someone crossing the border illegally would be caught and sent back, and the second was "deporting felons, not families," by focusing on deporting people who threaten public safety and national security—violent criminals, gang members, suspected terrorists, and people who have recently crossed the border.

The 2014 program was a companion to a 2012 program called Deferred Action for Childhood Arrivals, or DACA. Initially, it applied to immigrants thirty and under who had lived in the United States for at least five years before June of 2012 and had come here before they were sixteen. They had to pass a background check showing that they were in school, had graduated or obtained a certificate of completion from high school, had obtained a general education development certificate, or were an honorably discharged veteran of the Coast Guard or Armed Forces of the United States. They also had to show that they had not been convicted of a felony or other serious crime and did not pose a threat to public safety or national security. In 2014, the president expanded the 2012 program by saying an immigrant had to have lived in the United States since 2010 (rather than 2007), which made arrivals from three additional years eligible, and by extending the deferred action from two years to three so that the 2012 and 2014 programs would be in sync.

The legal authority for the new program, the Justice Department's Office of Legal Counsel advised, came from the Immigration and Nationality Act of 1952, which governs immigration and naturalization. The statute specified "which aliens may be removed from the United States and the procedures for doing so," a memo from the Office of Legal Counsel said. "As a general rule, when Congress vests enforcement authority in an executive agency, that agency has the discretion to decide whether a particular violation of the law warrants prosecution or other enforcement action." In 2012, in a major ruling about immigration, the Supreme Court had recognized that "the broad discretion exercised by immigration officials" is a "principal feature of the removal system."

This discretion had an obvious limit. As the memo noted, the executive branch "cannot, under the guise of exercising enforcement discretion, attempt to effectively rewrite the laws to match its policy preferences." But this limit had not been well defined in any Supreme Court decision. Because it could not be delineated easily, the memo went on, "the exercise of enforcement discretion generally is not subject to judicial review." Instead, "the political branches have addressed the proper allocation of enforcement authority through the political process."

On this issue, as on many others in the past two decades, the political process had been almost entirely ineffective. Congress had allocated only enough money for the Obama administration to deport about 400,000 people a year out of the 11.3 million immigrants who were in the country illegally. The administration's priorities reflected the constraint that Congress imposed— and the administration's decision to accept what the legal scholar Christina Rodriguez called Congress's "de facto delegation" of discretion. To the Obama administration, the program of Deferred Action for Parents of Americans, for which it said about 4 million people could qualify, reflected the broad discretion that the law allowed the executive branch in setting enforcement policy. But the size of the program, some senior officials recognized, made this use of discretion look aggressive, even though once they were confident they had the discretion, the program's size should be irrelevant.

The US government defined deferred action as an "act of administrative convenience to the government which gives some cases lower priority." For people who qualified, the lower priority would be the sole benefit conferred. It was strikingly flimsy: the government could revoke it the next day without warning, so it conferred no protection from being deported. It was not a pathway to citizenship or to any other substantive rights. It did not provide any degree of amnesty, which only Congress could do. Nor was the program even a typical exertion of executive power, because it did not depend on presidential authority provided by the Constitution. It was a matter of statutory interpretation, about the extent of the president's discretion in enforcing immigration law.

Obama political adversaries saw it otherwise, as "executive amnesty" that gave "legal status" to illegal immigrants, with their children functioning as "automatic human shields." That was how the complaint of the states saw it, too, in strikingly similar language. It declared that "the president of the United States announced that he would unilaterally suspend the immigration laws as applied to 4 million of the 11 million undocumented immigrants in the United States." The purpose of the order, "by executive fiat," was to "legalize the presence of approximately 40 percent of the known undocumented-immigrant population" and create "a de facto entitlement."

The US government's immigration policies under the Obama administration, the states went on, "have had and continue to have dire consequences in the Plaintiff States": "an enormous wave of undocumented immigrants" surging across the border, bringing "enormous law enforcement costs," with the Texas Department of Public Safety "spending $1.3 million a week on troopers and resources to deal with" the surge.

By exceeding the authority granted to the executive branch in federal statutes that govern immigration, the states continued, the administration had violated "the President's constitutional duty to 'take Care that the Laws be faithfully executed'" under the Constitution. As a result, it was already making a bad situation worse. The states asked Hanen to stop the program from going into effect and to declare it unconstitutional. Under the Administrative Procedure Act, which governs how agencies of the executive branch must propose and make rules, they asked the judge to rule that the program was unlawful in how it was made and in its substance.

In response, the US government said that the "Constitution and Congress have vested the Executive Branch, and the Secretary of Homeland Security in particular, with broad discretion over the enforcement of federal immigration law—including determining whether and when to remove (or not remove) particular aliens." The government, it went on, was enforcing the law—neither flouting it nor suspending it. The government had fulfilled obligations in statutes, followed priorities of Congress, and heeded humanitarian concerns of immigration laws to "emphasize national security, border security, and public safety" while "calling for the case-by-case exercise of deferred action—a long-established form of prosecutorial discretion—for certain low-priority aliens."

The level of enforcement was hard to quantify. The US government stopped using the term "deportation" in 1996. Since then, people prevented from entering the United States illegally ("excluded") and people expelled for being in the country illegally ("deported") were described in a new category—"removal." There were other categories of exclusion ("expedited removal," "return," "reinstatement") that made it difficult to total the number of people deported each year and compare that number to the reported annual total for previous administrations. Still, the Obama administration had deported so many people that advocates for immigrants icily called the president the deporter-in-chief.

In February of 2015, Hanen issued a 123-page opinion, which found that the government had "clearly legislated a substantive rule without complying with the procedural requirements under the Administration Procedure Act," because it had not given notice to the public about the rule while it was being developed and had not allowed time for comment about it. Based on that finding, Hanen issued an exceptionally broad injunction that barred the government from starting the program of deferred action anywhere in the United States rather than limiting the injunction to Texas or to the twenty-six states represented in the lawsuit. It also barred the government from carrying out the expansion of the related program of Deferred Action for Childhood Arrivals.

Federal district judges seldom write hundred-page opinions. When they do, it is usually to address a question about the meaning of the Constitution—not a failure to comply with the requirements of federal rulemaking. They even more seldom write opinions of that length before either side has had the opportunity to present evidence, or to challenge the evidence of the other side, and before there are facts accepted as evidence to which the judge can apply the law.

The heart of Hanen's opinion was the finding that the program of deferred action provided those who qualified for it with legal immigration status. He accepted the bumper-sticker version of the states' argument. Hanen called that status "legal presence," "legal status," and "legal presence status," as if each term was a synonym for legal immigration status.

They were not. In the netherworld of immigration law, "legal status" refers to the status of being accepted in the United States under federal law—as a documented immigrant, a nonimmigrant with a temporary visa, or someone on parole in the immigration system. The Obama executive order, the government said explicitly, did "not confer any form of legal status in this country," and the deferred action announced could "be terminated at any time at the agency's discretion."

Under a 1996 federal statute, "unlawful presence" is the status of immigrants who have not been formally admitted to the country or granted parole or who have stayed longer than the time they were granted. If someone is "unlawfully present" for more than six months but less than a year and leaves the country voluntarily, the person can apply to reenter the United States after waiting three years. If someone is unlawfully present for longer than a year, the person must wait a decade.

"Lawful presence" describes the circumstance of an immigrant lacking legal status when the government chooses not to enforce the law against him or her—as the government put it, "to countenance that person's continued presence in the United States" until it decides not to. Lawful presence does not mean legal presence. It is not a synonym for legal status. A person eligible for the new program was, by definition, unlawfully present in the United States. Every person covered by it would remain unlawfully present. The amount of time the person had already been unlawfully present would remain on his or her record. But his or her unlawful presence would stop accruing.

In May of 2015, by 2–1, the Fifth Circuit ruled in favor of the states, rejecting the appeal from the US government that the court overturn the injunction against both immigration programs, allowing one to begin and the other to expand. The essence of the majority opinion was that the injunction should stand because the states were likely to win on the merits in a trial. The opinion found that the new executive order's bestowal of "lawful presence" on immigrants illegally in the United States put a burden on the states, since that status made these immigrants eligible for accompanying benefits. Hanen had taken the first judicial step in turning politics into law. The majority for the appeals court took the second.

A dissent explained why that was wrong. In immigration law, it said, lawful status and lawful presence were not the same thing. The first was a status protected by law, which allows people with that status to stay in the United States. Congress had been explicit about how immigrants can gain that status. The second was the result of an official's exercise of discretion, which Congress had left to the attorney general or her designees, who could deport, anytime, people who were immigrants in the United States without lawful status. That included remaining without lawful status while benefitting from that discretion.

The dissent also explained why Hanen was wrong on the merits that the government had a duty under the Administrative Procedure Act to give the public notice about the new executive order and the chance to comment on it. Hanen held that the act required notice and comment in this case because the government's order told the Department of Homeland Security and the federal courts how to apply the order. That was wrong, the dissent said. The order was not binding: it set internal policy for the government yet left to immigration officers the discretion about how to apply the policy.

That was also wrong, the dissent said, because Hanen relied heavily on press statements of President Obama as a basis for concluding that the government was being disingenuous when it said that immigration officers should use their discretion in granting deferrals or not, depending on an individual's circumstances. Hanen had turned political statements, some taken out of context, into legal proof. The most damning statement of Obama, from when he was trying to cajole Congress into passing a major immigration reform bill, said that he didn't have the authority as president to do what the bill would grant. The dissent pointed out that the Supreme Court "has not relied on press statements to discern government motivation and test the legality of governmental action, much less inaction," because "presidents, like governors and legislators, often describe law enthusiastically yet defend the same law narrowly."

The tone of the dissent was measured. In the final paragraph, it said, "On the expedience of immigration measures, sensible things can be said on all sides, mindful that our country is an immigrant society itself." A footnote about that sentence said, "Over twenty years ago, Judith Shklar observed in her book *American Citizenship*, aptly subtitled *The Quest for Inclusion*, that the United States has an 'extremely complicated' history of 'exclusions and

inclusions, in which xenophobia, racism, religious big-
otry, and fear of alien conspiracies have played their part.'"

On the conservative Breitbart website the day the
appeals court decided the case, the opening paragraph of
an article reported that the dissent had "cited the country's
supposed history of racism and xenophobia," as if the dissent had said that was the whole American story rather than
an ugly part of it and as if that was the dissent's assertion,
not Shklar's idea. The spin of the opening paragraph underscored the political nature of the case. The Internet was busy
with similar spin. Supporters of the states treated the court
of public opinion as a crucial forum for their cause.

In November of 2015, also by 2–1, the Fifth Circuit again ruled for the states, this time on the question
of whether Hanen had abused his discretion in granting the preliminary injunction. Once again, the opinion
found that the new executive order's bestowal of "lawful
presence" on immigrants illegally in the United States
put a burden on the states, since that status made these
immigrants eligible for accompanying benefits. This time,
though, the explanation of the burden was more refined:
"The grant of lawful presence," the opinion said, "makes
otherwise ineligible persons eligible to qualify."

And the definition of lawful presence took account of
the counterview, so it sounded reasoned: "'Lawful presence' is not an enforceable right to remain in the United
States and can be revoked at any time, but that classification
nevertheless has significant legal consequences" because it
"awards lawful presence to persons who have never had a
legal status." The Fifth Circuit opinion was correct that "lawful presence" was not an enforceable right. The opinion was
correct that it could be revoked at any time. The opinion

was correct that "lawful presence" described people "who have never had a legal status." But the opinion was incorrect that the result was "significant legal consequences": an immigrant's lack of legal status combined with the person's continued lack of legal status, when the government chose not to deport the person today yet could deport the person tomorrow, did not have significant legal consequences in the positive sense that the opinion claimed.

The dissent pushed back on the majority's effort to equate lawful presence with legal status ("nothing in the Memorandum [the executive order] indicates that it is legally binding—i.e., that an applicant who is not granted deferred action can challenge that decision in court, or that DHS [the Department of Homeland Security] would be barred from removing an applicant who appears to satisfy the Memorandum's criteria"). But its more important point was about the nature of the lawsuit.

"The policy decisions at issue in this case are best resolved not by judicial fiat, but via the political process," the dissent said. "That this case essentially boils down to a policy dispute is underscored not only by the dozens of amicus briefs filed in this case by interested parties across the ideological spectrum—mayors, senators, representatives, and law enforcement officials, among others—but also by the district court's opinion, which repeatedly expresses frustration that the Secretary [of Homeland Security] is 'actively act[ing] to thwart' the immigration laws and 'is not just rewriting the laws [but] creating them from scratch.'"

The dissent in the previous Fifth Circuit case had made a similar point: "The political nature of this dispute is clear from the names on the briefs: hundreds of mayors, police chiefs, sheriffs, attorneys general, governors, and state legislators—not to mention 185 members of Congress, 15 states and the District of Columbia on the one hand, and 113 members of Congress and 26 states on the other."

The point of both dissents was that disputes about immigration, and about this kind of immigration issue, are for the political branches to resolve—and it is not the role of the judiciary to step in if, for example, the House of Representatives chooses not to vote on a bipartisan and comprehensive bill passed by the Senate that would have resolved the dispute.

From the perspective of both dissents, that is what Hanen did in the District Court and what the Fifth Circuit majorities did as well. The judges in the lower courts reflected the views of the political party of the president who had appointed them. Democrats had appointed the dissenters from the two different appellate decisions. (Obama appointed Stephen Higginson; Jimmy Carter appointed Carolyn Dineen King.) Republicans had appointed the judges supporting the lawsuit. (George W. Bush appointed Hanen, the trial judge; Ronald Reagan appointed Jerry E. Smith, who wrote both majority opinions; and George W. Bush appointed Jennifer Walker Elrod, who joined both appellate opinions.)

It was a great stroke of luck for the challengers of the Obama program that the Republican-appointed judges heard both parts of the appeal. The Fifth Circuit's system for assigning cases randomly gave them to those two conservative judges both times: first to review the likelihood of the success of the motion for the injunction so it made sense to end the injunction or put it into effect and second to consider the merits of the motion.

The policy dispute had moved to the federal court because Republican state leaders wanted it to. The split between judges appointed by Democrats versus those appointed by Republicans made the legal controversy feel political, as it was. That made the Republicans' redefinition of lawful presence into legal status look like a political judgment rather than a legal one, in light of the interpretation to the contrary of past administrations and courts. The timing of the second Fifth Circuit decision reinforced this impression. It came out more than five months after the first decision and three months after the oral argument in the case, even though the second three-judge panel included two of the three judges from the first panel who knew the case well.

That left little time for the Obama administration to ask the Supreme Court to review and decide the case in the 2015 term. The states asked the Court for extra time to file their brief with the Court. If the Court had granted the motion, it would not have been able to hear the case until the next Court term. The justices denied the request. In the last Court meeting where that was possible, they took the case for review in April of 2016.

The morning the Supreme Court heard the argument, the plaza in front of the Court was a carnival of demonstrators—most, it seemed, in favor of the president's executive order being reviewed by the Court. The line of immigrants who would be affected by the Court's ruling and of their supporters wrapped behind the building. That made the crowd appear larger than the one almost exactly a year before, when the Court heard the argument about whether the Constitution requires a state to recognize a marriage between two people of the same sex. And larger even than the crowds four years earlier when, for three days, the Court heard arguments about whether Congress had the authority under the Constitution to pass the Affordable Care Act—Obamacare—in 2010.

The gathering this April morning was a political event: raucous, colorful, and animated by worry as well as hope. The crowd included opponents of the executive order, too, and of immigration in general. Police kept the tension in relative check. Each side kept the other's good cheer in check. With the magnitude of the crowd and everyone's reason for being there, it was almost surprising not to see giant speakers mounted on the building so people outside could hear the oral argument as it happened inside the courtroom.

Inside the courtroom, there were only eight justices because Justice Scalia had died two months before. The division in the Court between four conservatives and four liberals reinforced the view of the press, Supreme Court bar members, and other insiders that this was a political case. It took less than a minute into the argument of Donald B. Verrilli Jr., the solicitor general of the United States, for the audience to be reminded that while the justices couldn't hear what was happening outside, they were aware of the extraordinary public interest in the controversy and of their power to decide whether to deal with its substance or not.

Chief Justice Roberts said, "General, maybe it would make logical progression if you began with your 'standing' argument first." "Standing" is the legal term meaning that a plaintiff has a basis for bringing a lawsuit. In this case, the primary claim Texas made was that under the program for parents, at least half a million immigrants would become eligible for driver's licenses, because under Texas law, an immigrant may apply for a license if he presents "documentation issued by the appropriate United States agency that authorizes the applicant to be in the United States," and the state said that anyone receiving "deferred action" under the new federal policy would qualify. That would cost the state millions of dollars, Texas said, because it charges each person who gets a license less than each one costs the state. That was a concrete injury, Texas argued, traceable to the new policy of the federal government and likely to be remedied by a favorable decision for the states—the requirements for standing.

In its petition to the Court asking the justices to overturn the Fifth Circuit, the US government contended that accepting Texas's argument meant that any state could create its own standing to challenge a federal policy, which Texas had done in this case by voluntarily deciding "to provide a state subsidy" to the immigrants that the parents' program benefitted. That choice by Texas was the cause of any injury to the state, the US government said, not the new federal policy.

"Standing" is a rarefied concept. In 1961, the legal scholar Alexander M. Bickel gave it prominence in the *Harvard Law Review* in an essay called "The Passive Virtues." He argued that, as the unelected branch in the federal government that had a critical role in resolving controversies where politics intersected with law, the judiciary, especially justices of the Supreme Court, should preserve their limited political capital for use in controversies they had to decide by not deciding those they did not. As former Acting Solicitor General Walter E. Dellinger III, during the Clinton administration, reminded the justices in the immigration case in a friend-of-the-Court brief, "This Court draws much of its legitimacy from deciding *not* to decide," especially when the public "'is currently engaged in an active political debate over'" the subject addressed in the lawsuit.

That quote in Dellinger's brief about the "active political debate" was from the first line of a 2013 opinion for the Court by the chief justice, in which it decided not to address then whether the Constitution requires the states to recognize same-sex marriage. In 1993, after he had completed a widely admired four-year stint in the first Bush administration as principal deputy solicitor general, Roberts published a law-review essay that made an eloquent case for this kind of narrow interpretation of standing. Referring to the part of the Constitution setting out the authority of the federal judiciary, he wrote, "The legitimacy of an unelected, life-tenured judiciary in our democratic republic is bolstered by the constitutional limitation of that judiciary's power in Article III to actual 'cases' and 'controversies.'" He went on, "Standing is thus properly regarded as a doctrine of judicial self-restraint."

Dellinger's brief went on to explain: "Given the political electricity pulsing through this case, the Court must take extra care to determine whether it is a 'Case' that can be decided by the federal judiciary, and, even if so, whether any cause of action provides a basis for review. Application of long-settled principles yields but one answer to those questions: no." He added, "To hold otherwise would not only inject the Court into this political maelstrom, but also the next one, and the next." The brief for the US government made a related point: the appeals court's rulings saying that Texas and the other states had standing to sue "threaten[ed] a vast expansion of the judicial power that would entangle federal courts in policy disputes that are properly resolved through the political process."

During the oral argument at the Supreme Court, Roberts said to Verrilli, "And as I understand from your brief, your answer is, 'Well, just don't give them driver's licenses.'" The solicitor general (or SG) started to answer the chief justice, but three other justices jumped in, and the SG needed to answer them, too. Eventually, Roberts followed up like this: "Their argument is," referring to the states, "'We're going to give a driver's license to people subject to deferred action.' And you're saying, 'Okay, that's your injury? You can take that away.' And I just think that's a real Catch-22. 'If you're injured, you have standing. But you're not injured, because you can change your policy and not give driver's licenses to these people.' And I suggest that I think you would sue them instantly if they said that."

If his hypothetical situation occurred and Texas said it would not give a driver's license to anyone in the program, the government's position, the chief suggested, would be, "'People here lawfully present under the federal authority are being discriminated against.'" With that sentence, Roberts sent two important signals: first, he was not persuaded by the government's view of standing in this case and, sympathetic to the states' view, he was eager for the Court to decide this political case; and second, by using a version of the most loaded term in the case, "lawfully present," he revealed that he was inclined to take the states' side in resolving it.

An exchange not long after in the oral argument strengthened this impression (the "Guidance" he referred to next was the Obama administration's explanation about the legal issues raised by the immigration program):

Roberts: I have to ask you about two pages in your reply brief. On page sixteen, you quote the Guidance that says, "The individuals covered are lawfully present in the United States." And less than a page later, you say, "Aliens with deferred action are present in violation of the law."

Now, that must have been a hard sentence to write. I mean, they're—they're lawfully present, and yet, they're present in violation of the law.

Verrilli: I actually had no trouble write it, Mr. Chief Justice.

(Laughter.)

Verrilli: The reason I had no problem writing it is because that phrase, "lawful presence," has caused a terrible amount of confusion in this case; I realize it. But the reality is it means—it means something different to people in the immigration world.

What it means in the immigration world is not that you have a legal right to be in the United States, that your status has changed in any way. That you have any defense to removal. It doesn't mean any of those things, and it never has. And—and so it doesn't—and so at that fundamental level, we are not trying to change anybody's legal status on the immigration—

Roberts: Lawfully present does not mean you're legally present in the United States.

Verrilli: Right. Tolerated—

Roberts: I'm sorry, that—just so I get that right.

Verrilli: Yes.

Roberts: Lawfully present does not mean that you're legally present.

Verrilli: Correct.

In an opinion column for the *New York Times* the week after the argument, Linda Greenhouse chided Roberts and Justice Samuel Alito, who had joined the chief in that line of inquiry during the oral argument, for playing dumb. She wrote, "It turns out that the phrase 'lawful presence,' understood as a term embedded in the labyrinth of statutes, regulations, and practice of immigration law, doesn't have the obvious meaning it would have in everyday speech, namely, that someone is in the country legally and has the right to remain here. Is that really so hard for two of the top lawyers in the United States to understand?"

She also predicted how the case would turn out: "The general takeaway from last week's argument was that the administration is going to lose by a 4-to-4 tie. A tie affirms the lower court, and because tie votes don't result in opinions (the Justices on either side of the tie are not even identified), the court in that scenario would hand the administration a stinging defeat while sparing the Justices the bother of having to explain themselves."

Two months later, the Court did what Greenhouse predicted, issuing this brief opinion: "The judgment is affirmed by an equally divided Court." The Fifth Circuit's decision stood and with it, Judge Hanen's injunction throughout the United States against Deferred Action for Parents of Americans and Lawful Permanent Residents. The next step in the lawsuit would be a Justice Department motion for a rehearing by the justices once the Senate confirmed a ninth justice—whenever that happened.

A case about the most ideologically charged subject in American life turned into one in which politics and law could not be differentiated, making law seem like another venue of politics and the judges who made the legal decisions seem like politicians in robes.

"This Court draws much of its legitimacy from deciding *not* to decide," Dellinger had written. It also depletes that legitimacy when it decides to decide and the reasons are not explained yet seem to be partisan. It depletes that legitimacy when it decides to decide and it cannot.

The Court said nothing about its division in this case—who the justices were on each side, what they disagreed about, and why. It failed to provide what distinguishes it from the other branches: legal reasons. But a safe bet was that, as the lower court judges were, the justices of the Supreme Court were evenly divided between those appointed by Republicans and those appointed by Democrats. A few weeks later, Justice Ruth Bader Ginsburg gave an interview to the *New York Times* in which she seemed to confirm that.

Adam Liptak recounted for the *Times* that the 4–4 deadlock "left in place a nationwide injunction blocking Mr. Obama's plan to spare more than four million unauthorized immigrants from deportation and allow them to work. That was unfortunate, Justice Ginsburg said, but it could have been worse. 'Think what would have happened had Justice Scalia remained with us,' she said. Instead of a single sentence announcing the tie, she suggested, a five-Justice majority would have issued a precedent-setting decision dealing a lasting setback to Mr. Obama and the immigrants he had tried to protect."

It was an indiscreet revelation about the Court's decision. But the burst of media attention to the justice's entry into American presidential politics through her comments about Donald Trump eclipsed it.

C h a p t e r 2

A Political Institution

The white marble of the Supreme Court building is veined with mica that shimmers in sunlight. It projects ageless dignity and high importance. With imposing columns and a grand facade, it looks like a temple of justice, as it was meant to. At the ceremony in 1932 when the building's cornerstone was laid on Capitol Hill in Washington, DC, Chief Justice Charles Evans Hughes linked the timelessness of the architecture to what he called the "imperishable ideal of liberty under law."

A pair of giant bronze doors picks up that theme, with four panels arrayed vertically on each door depicting "The Evolution of Justice" in sculptures elevated from the background. They begin with a scene that Homer described in the *Iliad* where two men argue a point of primitive law. The real point is that in peacetime, the law prohibits killing, and disputes must be settled in court. They end with Chief Justice John Marshall and Justice Joseph Story—who served together for twenty-four years in the early nineteenth century and remain giants in Court history—discussing the landmark 1803 ruling in *Marbury v. Madison*. In that decision, Marshall pronounced the

Court's role as the ultimate authority on the meaning of the Constitution.

The timelessness of the building, coupled with the evolution of justice as the art portrays it, conveys Hughes's ideal. The Court stands as the ultimate authority in American law, in the spirit of the great lawgivers shown in the building's facade, like Moses for the Hebrews and Hammurabi for the Babylonians. The law evolves, yet the Court ensures its constancy, as the guardian of order and beacon of liberty in American life.

The building embodies the ideal of law as noble and set apart in a nation that prides itself on its fidelity to the law's rule. In contrast to the dealings of Congress, transacted in the United States Capitol across the street, or to the business of the executive branch, carried out below the Capitol in the buildings along Pennsylvania Avenue leading to the White House, the Supreme Court building embodies the ideal of the Court as an arbiter of law above the fray of politics.

In October of 1935, however, when the building opened and justices first heard arguments in their ornate new courtroom, no one with a modicum of knowledge about American law and politics believed that about the Court. About the building and its incarnation of law, most of the justices found the whole thing grandiose. One called it "almost bombastically pretentious." Rather than embrace the theme of its art, they fixated on some of the mortals unexpectedly chosen to embody the ideal of law as models for sculptures on the building, including its architect, Cass Gilbert, and, apparently without his blessing, Hughes himself.

The Supreme Court had sought to nullify the New Deal since soon after its start in 1933, when Hughes administered the presidential oath to Franklin D. Roosevelt. Following the Court's lead, in 1935 and '36, wrote Robert Jackson, from his perspective as attorney general, before he became a justice, "over a hundred district judges each had assumed the power to nullify acts of Congress"—five out of every eight judges of the approximately 160 serving across the United States at the time. They issued 1,600 injunctions to restrain the federal government from carrying out just one of the many federal statutes the Court soon nullified. They issued many more about other new statutes.

The political fight was over whether the Constitution gave the elected executive and legislative branches the power to rescue the United States from the Great Depression after the Democrats got an overwhelming mandate to do that: FDR won in a landslide, the biggest in American history, and the Democrats won strong majorities in both houses of Congress. The political branches were trying to respond to the Depression by stimulating the economy and bringing its excesses under control through a major expansion of the role of the federal government and of the regulation of business, finance, labor, and other elements of the economy and society.

The Court, Jackson wrote, was "deep in power politics" and was denying "important powers to both state and nation." The Court was the great foe of FDR. He had said so frankly when campaigning to be president in 1932. It was carrying on a struggle that went back half a century, from the decades after the Civil War when the country began to evolve from an agricultural society into an urban industrialized one. The Court kept the government from regulating labor by enforcing the freedom of organizations

41

and workers to make contracts with each other. It kept the government from regulating goods and services in the economy by protecting businesses from infringement on their property rights.

"When judges ruled against protective legislation or restrictions on property rights," the legal historian Melvin I. Urofsky wrote, "they claimed that they were not making policy or law but merely applying the proper rule. Abstract reasoning, deliberate ignorance of the facts of industrial society, a limited role for the state, and a belief in immutable law combined with an emphasis on individualism to make up classical legal thought."

By the time of the Depression, however, it was clear to many that the Court was making policy as well as law when it struck down New Deal legislation. The Depression happened for a host of reasons: the stock market crash in which the Dow Jones Industrial Average lost 90 percent of its value, the failures of over nine thousand banks, and other massive breakdowns in the laissez-faire economy. The Court had long protected laissez-faire and was implicated in this catastrophe. Jackson wrote, "The basic grievance of the New Deal was that the Court has seemed unduly to favor private economic power and always to find ways of circumventing the efforts of popular government to control or regulate it."

The historian Jeff Shesol summarized in *Supreme Power: Franklin Roosevelt versus the Supreme Court*, "By 1937, the Court's majority had made amply clear that the very notion of the New Deal—its use of governmental power to relieve the suffering caused by the Great Depression and to create a new and more just social and economic order—was an affront to the Constitution, whether that power was exercised by the federal government or the states. The Court, Roosevelt complained to the press, had established a 'no-man's-land' where no government—state or federal—can function."

This was a full-blown constitutional crisis.

In February of 1937, FDR made a combative proposal for another new federal statute—this one targeting the Court. Under it, when a justice of the Supreme Court reached seventy and chose not to retire, the president would appoint a new justice with the advice and consent of the Senate. While he proposed capping the size of the Court at fifteen, compared with the nine it had been for sixty-eight years, that would allow him to appoint a new justice for each of the six justices then over seventy if he did not retire.

FDR sought to pack the Court. Privately, in his "circle of court-packers," as one called it, that was his blunt purpose. To the public, though, he insisted that he had no such intention, in the sense of appointing "spineless puppets who would disregard the law and would decide specific cases as I wished them to be decided." Instead, he pledged to "appoint Justices who will not undertake to override the judgment of the Congress on legislative policy." Congress had the power to change the Court's size, he reminded. It had gone from six justices in 1789 to five in 1801, then seven in 1807, nine in 1837, ten in 1863, seven again in 1866, and back to nine in 1869.

The president said his goals were to "make the administration of all Federal justice speedier and, therefore, less costly" and to "save our national Constitution from hardening of the judicial arteries." The proposal applied to every federal court. Any president would have the authority under FDR's proposal, with the advice and consent of the Senate, to appoint new trial and appeals-court judges when current ones reached seventy and did not retire.

Citing "overcrowded Federal dockets" as a pretext, his proposal purported neither to focus on the Supreme Court nor to criticize its intransigence. But the pretext fooled nobody. Categorizing the plan as the deepest threat to American governance since the secession of southern states that precipitated the Civil War, the columnist Walter Lippmann called it "a bloodless coup d'état."

The plan famously backfired. Robert Jackson wrote, "Instead of accusing some Justices of being stubbornly and wrongly reactionary, which the other Justices could hardly deny, the message in effect charged the Justices collectively with inefficiency and inadequate discharge of duty." Justice Louis D. Brandeis, the Court's elder statesman, joined Hughes "in a letter hotly denying the whole thesis of the message so far as the Supreme Court was concerned."

In early March of 1937, FDR gave a fireside chat on the radio to rally support for his proposal. He put aside his coyness. The Court had been functioning as "a policy-making body," "a third House of Congress," and "a super-legislature," he said, and America had "reached the point as a nation where we must take action to save the Constitution from the Court and the Court from itself." But the plan "never lived down its initial indirection," Jackson judged, and Congress rejected it outright. With a 70–20 vote, the Senate buried the bill by returning it to the Senate Judiciary Committee.

FDR was the happy victor, however. Justice Owen Roberts, on the Court since 1930, joined Hughes as a swing vote between four conservative opponents of the New Deal and three liberals who generally supported it. The Republican President Herbert Hoover had appointed Roberts after the Senate rejected a previous choice for the seat. In 1936, he voted with the conservatives to strike down a New York State minimum-wage law. A year later in the *Parrish* case, he switched sides, joining the liberals (and the chief justice, who wrote the opinion) to uphold a similar Washington State minimum-wage law—and, in another case, striking down a major fourteen-year-old precedent that held that a District of Columbia minimum-wage law was "an arbitrary interference with the liberty of contract which no government can legally justify in a free land."

Roberts's reversal is famous as "the switch in time that saved nine," as if FDR's plan for the judiciary and the threat of swelling the Court to fifteen members had prompted the justice to understand the crisis that the Court had created by nullifying the New Deal and to change his allegiance. In a memorandum he wrote in 1945, near the end of his tenure, Roberts disputed that view. He said that the case had been argued in December of 1936, that he had cast his vote then—before FDR announced his plan—and that "no action taken by the president in the interim had any causal relation to my action in the *Parrish* case."

In mid-April of 1937, on the other hand, when Roberts's switch became apparent with the Supreme Court's announcement of decisions, an observer at the Court said that he looked as if he "had been through hell." Roberts later spoke about "the tremendous strain" that he (and the Court) had been under. As Jeff Shesol chronicled, Roberts had made a slow and vexing change in his outlook, from orthodox thinking about the limited power of Congress and the states to regulate the economy, to the flexible view of the New Deal. The four conservative justices, Shesol wrote, "considered Roberts gone for good—and with him the fight for all they believed in."

Hughes had led where Roberts followed, dramatically in an opinion for the new liberal majority of five, which rebuked the conservative four for asking that the Court and the nation "shut our eyes to the plainest facts of our national life." (About a 1946 interview he did with Roberts, Hughes's biographer Merlo J. Pusey recorded in his notes: "Roberts says Hughes is a towering personality—the most orderly and astute mind he has encountered.")

What seemed to pain Roberts apparently made Hughes feel triumphant, as the savior of the Court and even of the nation. Hughes was known as an incisive moderate who, in a detached manner, paid close attention to each case's facts as well as to the relevant law. In an impartial, nonideological way, he had sought to serve as a balance between the Court's conservatives and liberals. But the cleavage on the Court had become so debilitating that Hughes decided he must address it in a different way.

In his book *FDR and Chief Justice Hughes*, James F. Simon described a visit that Hughes made in the summer of 1936, when the Court was not in session, to the Pennsylvania country home of Roberts. According to Simon, Hughes "used several of those hours to engage his colleague in intense conversation." There is apparently no record of what they talked about, Simon wrote, "But critical agreement between the two Justices in several important decisions during the next Court term suggests that their summer discussion covered more than the joys of vacation."

Between 1937 and 1944, the Supreme Court reduced protection for economic claims and expanded national power, creating a new framework for government under the Constitution now called the modern administrative state. It overturned about four precedents a year in that span, compared with about one precedent every four years from 1810 until the Roberts switch. Jackson wrote, "The Court's abuse of its powers had called forth the Court plan; an awakened sense of judicial self-restraint and self-discipline removed its urgent need." He went on, "In politics the black-robed reactionary Justices had won over the master liberal politician of our day. In law the president defeated the recalcitrant Justices in their own Court."

Politics and law were tautly intertwined and sometimes indistinguishable. The Court was a central concern of politics in the nation's capital but also around the country. Court rulings directly affected the well-being of the nation with wide political impacts. Competing views about law and the meaning of the Constitution had profoundly divided the Court: politics brought about a resolution. In addition to being *of* politics, the Court was *in* politics as well. The elegant vision of law as above the fray of politics, exemplified by the Court's neoclassical building and its metaphorical art, was fundamentally at odds with the inelegant reality that shaped major rulings of the justices.

G. Edward White, in *The American Judicial Tradition*, explained that "American Justices have been expected to demonstrate that their decisions, despite often having major political consequences, are faithful to law as opposed to partisan ideology." Before the switch in time, the New Deal Court was a throwback to the nineteenth century, when the dominant view was that justices found law in a body of legal principles. An overarching one was the Court's duty to protect private property rights against unlawful government regulation or worse—corruption and even tyranny. In the constitutional system of checks and balances, White wrote, the old Court's function was to protect "American citizens against the demagogic tendencies of popular bodies." The law was the primary restraint on justices, as "an external, immanent, timeless causal agent in the universe."

The resolution of the constitutional crisis marked the beginning of the Court's modern era. There has been an almost continuous debate ever since about the proper role of the Court and the justices, based on a very different belief. A central premise has been that justices make law, they do not find it, so the law on its own is an insufficient constraint. The primary one, to conservatives and liberals, has been institutional—the Court's role as an institution of government in American democracy.

For much of this period, conservatives have promoted the idea of judicial restraint, or self-restraint, which liberals like Justices Oliver Wendell Holmes and Louis D. Brandeis supported in the early twentieth century as a counter to the Court's aggressive rejection of social and economic legislation and as a constraint on the inevitable influence of a judge's ideological views. The Court, by and large, needed to defer to the decisions of Congress and the president as democratically elected representatives, the argument has gone.

Liberals did not abandon judicial restraint: under the influence of Holmes and Brandeis, they continued to regard it generally as the proper and professional approach of a judge, regardless of ideology. But liberals developed exceptions to restraint when they felt it was the Court's duty to recognize rights under the Constitution that the democratic branches were hindering, sometimes crushing—especially rights of minorities.

In the most important footnote in American constitutional law, in 1938, Justice Harlan Fiske Stone (FDR picked him to succeed Hughes as chief in 1941) distinguished between statutes dealing with economic and social welfare legislation and those dealing with "the very essence of ordered liberty." Stone wrote that "the presumption of constitutionality" should be set aside and that legislation should be "subjected to more exacting judicial scrutiny" when it "restricts those political processes which can ordinarily be expected to bring about repeal of undesirable legislation" or when it is "directed at particular religious, or national, or racial minorities"—"against discrete and insular minorities" who are victims of "prejudice."

As the University of Chicago's David Strauss put it in a 2009 lecture, the "footnote was the Court's first—and maybe only—attempt to say, systematically, when the courts should declare laws unconstitutional." The idea at the heart of the footnote blossomed into the Court's robust protection of equality in the 1950s and '60s under Chief Justice Earl Warren and into its arrival as a national institution providing uniform standards of fairness in a wide range of legal areas. Conservatives attacked this body of cases as the results of judicial activism—even rootless activism. Liberals countered that in general, the Court was protecting the workings of democracy, sometimes by protecting groups that the political process had shut out.

Nineteen-sixty-eight was a fateful year for the Court and for American justice. Warren told President Lyndon B. Johnson he was ready to retire. Johnson sought to replace him with Justice Abe Fortas, a liberal former New Dealer who was a longtime adviser to the president and who had continued to play that role after Johnson put him on the Court. Opponents who wanted to keep him from becoming chief because of his liberalism went after him for his continuing advice to Johnson, for violating the separation of powers between the branches. Johnson eventually asked that Fortas's nomination be withdrawn after senators learned that for teaching a summer course, he was paid $15,000 (in 2016 dollars, about $108,000)—an increase of almost 40 percent over his $39,500 salary as a justice. (It is now common for justices to be paid well for short-term teaching, but they must disclose that income.)

The following year, Fortas resigned from the Court when *Life* magazine published an exposé about his dealings with a financier and corporate raider, Louis Wolfson, who was a former client of Fortas's. In 1966, while Fortas was on the Court, Wolfson had paid the Justice $20,000 as a consultant to his charitable foundation. Fortas returned the money when Wolfson was indicted for selling unregistered shares of stock and for perjury and obstruction of justice. He was convicted.

During Fortas's confirmation hearing to become chief justice in 1968, senators had criticized him and the Warren Court for being soft on crime at a moment when crime was increasing in the United States. Richard Nixon made law-and-order a big theme of his campaign to be president, and that helped get him elected. By 1971, he got the opportunity to fill four seats on the Supreme Court. Instead of the liberal Fortas, he selected the conservative Warren E. Burger to become chief justice in 1969, the first of the three conservative chief justices from then until now, picked by Republican presidents—after Burger, William H. Rehnquist and then John G. Roberts Jr. Counting the chiefs, Republicans picked twelve out of the past sixteen justices.

In the Court's modern era, there has been increasing evidence from political science (and increasing acceptance of it), that ideology plays a significant part in how justices decide cases. Beginning in the Reagan administration, Republicans increasingly attacked what they believed they were replacing: the activism of the Warren Court. They made this cause concrete with an agenda they set out for the Court: making criminal law tougher, reducing the size of the national government and returning power to the states, ending abortion rights, ending affirmative action, bringing religious prayer back to public schools, and more.

They launched the Federalist Society to promote this agenda and create a cadre of young conservatives to pursue it. They made it one of the country's most influential legal organizations. Leaders of this movement, like Robert Bork, the onetime Yale Law School professor who became a judge on the US Court of Appeals for the District of Columbia Circuit and an unsuccessful nominee to the Supreme Court, derided landmark rulings of the Warren Court as corrupt constitutional law. With that pejorative, they gave themselves license to attack and overturn it.

Heroes of the movement embraced originalism, the belief that the primary constraint on justices was how they should interpret the Constitution, not the institutional role of the Court. The main tenets were that the meaning of America's fundamental law did not change over time and that justices were obliged to figure out and apply the meaning that the document had for its framers and their contemporaries through analysis of the constitutional text and history.

The Constitution was not a living document, as Republicans and Democrats in the previous generation had generally agreed. It was, Justice Scalia delighted in repeating, "dead, dead, dead." He argued, "The only good Constitution is a dead Constitution. The problem with a living Constitution in a word is that somebody has to decide how it grows and when it is that new rights are—you know—come forth."

On the Supreme Court in the past generation, Scalia and Clarence Thomas were the only justices to embrace originalism. In 2001, Jack Balkin of Yale Law School explained its limits in a book called *Living Originalism.* He recognized that Scalia's brand of originalism was useful in underscoring the importance of the Constitution's text and history as sources of its meaning, which justices and legal scholars since the start of the republic had emphasized. But when the terms of the text were broad, Balkin showed, like "equal protection of the laws," the original meaning was general. The specific meaning of the text—the meaning to be applied in future circumstances—had to depend on American experience, in life as well as law.

Brown v. Board of Education is often called the most important Supreme Court decision in the twentieth century. In that case, in 1954, the Court ruled that segregation in public schools is unconstitutional. Under originalism as Scalia understood it, there was no basis for the decision in the Constitution. Yet the decision was unanimous, based on wide agreement among its supporters as well as critics, that the justices had to make a decision resting on values as much as on law. It is impossible to overstate the unrest the ruling triggered in the legal culture and around the country. It continues to reverberate, in politics and law, with the current consensus, articulated by Harvard Law School's Michael Klarman, that the ruling's immediate impact was to impede racial progress because of the backlash it stirred in the South.

In 1957, a group of scholars gathered to address the "crisis of Court and Constitution" that *Brown* led to and the role of the Court as a legal institution with a central part in politics. The political scientist Robert A. Dahl explained why, in his view, that was not a cause for concern: the Court was a political institution as well as a legal one, he wrote, because "from time to time its members decide cases where legal criteria are not in any realistic sense adequate to the task."

Dahl recognized that "[a]s a political institution, the Court is highly unusual, not least because Americans are not quite willing to accept the fact that it is a political institution and not quite capable of denying it; so that frequently we take both positions at once. This is confusing to foreigners, amusing to logicians, and rewarding to ordinary Americans who thus manage to retain the best of both worlds."

The Court's occasional political decisions rarely rocked American democracy, Dahl said, because for the most part, those rulings were in tune with the views of the majority: "Indeed, it is not too much to say that if

Justices were appointed primarily for their 'judicial' qualities without regard to their basic attitudes on fundamental questions of public policy, the Court could not play the influential role in the American political system that it does in reality play."

From 1916 until 1954, of the twenty-five men nominated for the Supreme Court who were confirmed and served, only five had answered questions at a Senate hearing. But when President Dwight D. Eisenhower nominated John M. Harlan II to the Court in 1955, southern Democrats and others on the Senate Judiciary Committee who opposed the school-desegregation ruling saw a way to delay desegregation: they would ask him questions at a confirmation hearing. Harlan was then a judge on the US Court of Appeals for the Second Circuit in New York City, so they called him to testify about his views on legal issues as a candidate for a Court where the members were, from some committee members' perspectives, voting based on their personal views and not on the dictates of the law. Every nominee from Harlan through Elena Kagan, except for some whose nominations were withdrawn, has been asked to testify—about thirty nominees in sixty years. It was Harlan's nomination that turned the confirmation process into a political event.

In these years, as G. Edward White wrote, "The tradeoff between independence and accountability" still seemed central "to defining the appellate judicial role." But while the justices of the Supreme Court retained their independence under the Constitution, what were once seen as firm constraints holding the justices accountable had all fallen away: the law as found and not made, the Court's limited role in American democracy, and the original meaning of the Constitution. The main constraint left was politics, which, by 2015, most observers recognized was broken.

By the beginning of the Supreme Court's 2015 term, there was no doubt that Chief Justice Roberts wanted the Court to be respected as an institution of government distinct from the executive and legislative branches, standing, as he put it, "outside the political arena." He had used the "iconic monument" of the eighty-year-old Court building, with its "classical elements and durable stone," as a proxy for the institution's "imperishable role in our system of government." He was using his admiration for Charles Evans Hughes as chief justice to reinforce his concept of "a strong, independent, and impartial Judiciary," especially the Supreme Court.

In his view, Hughes protected the Court's independence by defeating FDR's Court-packing plan—in Roberts's words, the cause of one of the Court's "greatest crises." In November of 2015, Roberts told the Historical Society of the New York Courts, "It fell to Hughes to guide a very unpopular Supreme Court through that high-noon showdown against America's most popular president since George Washington."

Roberts stressed the importance of how Hughes defeated the plan. "Hughes appreciated that that would be sort of fighting the battle on the enemy's turf," Roberts said, because FDR was a charismatic politician, and the battle was happening in Congress, the most political of the branches. Hughes was a former governor of New York and Secretary of State who had come within a couple thousand votes in California of being elected president in 1916 and who, in FDR's view, was the best politician in the country. He worked "under the radar," providing Congress with facts and reasons that refuted the plan rather than challenging the president's rhetoric about the Court and Constitution.

But Roberts did not address what most consider the more important outcome of the crisis—the end of conservative domination of the Court in 1937. By focusing on Hughes's part in the political struggle in Congress rather than on the transformation that politics brought about in the Court's rulings, the chief justice maintained the framework for understanding the distinction between law and politics that he presented during his confirmation hearing as a prospective justice.

In one sense, the Court with Roberts as chief justice simply continued the conservative orientation of the Court under his predecessor Rehnquist and, before him, Burger. Compared with the Court when Earl Warren was chief justice, from 1953 to 1969, the Court under Republican-picked chief justices since then had been notably more conservative, even though it made landmark decisions that were liberal and had been by no means consistently either ideological or conservative.

But the Roberts Court had been more conservative still. The scholar Lee Epstein told me, "On the Burger and Rehnquist Courts, in non-unanimous decisions, Justices appointed by Republican presidents voted for liberal outcomes 42 percent of the time, those appointed by Democrats, 64 percent. On the Roberts Court, it's been 39 percent and 71 percent, with the gap much more pronounced. That tells me that there is an alignment according to partisanship and ideology."

The justices regularly divided along those lines. The press described them as doing that often enough for the schism to define the Roberts Court, which dismayed the chief justice. Early in February of 2016, in a public conversation in Boston with the dean of New England Law School, Roberts said, "We don't work as Democrats or Republicans." He blamed the misperception that they did on the confirmation process—the process of the Senate for considering nominees for the Court. He said, "When you have a sharply political, divisive hearing process, it increases the danger that whoever comes out of it will be viewed in those terms. If the Democrats and Republicans have been fighting so fiercely about whether you're going to be confirmed, it's natural for some members of the public to think that you must be identified in a particular way."

Ten days later, Antonin Scalia, appointed by President Ronald Reagan in 1986 and a member of the Court for almost thirty years, died unexpectedly. His death set off a chain of events that made plain that the challenge for the chief justice was not solely the hearing process, though the process is as rancorous as Roberts described. The challenge for the chief intent on leading a legal institution, standing outside politics, was that the Court is also a political one—and even when the justices are intent on making a legal decision, politics in the form of ideology regularly plays a significant role.

After Scalia's death, when Mitch McConnell and Charles Grassley announced that the 2016 presidential election should decide who selected Scalia's replacement, they rested their view on historical practice: since the second term of FDR's presidency, or for the previous eighty years, they said, no president had filled a Court vacancy in an election year.

In the *New York University Law Review*, Robin Bradley Kar and Jason Mazzone, professors at the University of Illinois College of Law, called that and other Republican accounts "partial, misleading, or erroneous." They wrote that "the Republican plan is historically unprecedented." Its "logical terminus," they said, may be that "no future Supreme Court Justice will be appointable unless the president and the Senate are of the same political party." That result, they went on, "can only lead to a more—rather than less—politicized appointment process and, ultimately, to a more politicized Court."

They examined "every Supreme Court appointment process in U.S. history" and concluded that the Senate may do what the Republicans were doing only "if there are contemporaneous questions about the status of the nominating president as the most recently elected president"— because he was elected vice-president and ascended to the White House after the president died, for example, or because he made the nomination after his successor was elected. Otherwise, they found 103 cases in which "an elected president nominated someone to fill an actual Supreme Court vacancy and began the nomination process prior to the election of a successor." In all of them, going "back all the way to the earliest days of the republic, the sitting president was able to both nominate *and appoint* a replacement Justice—by and with the advice and consent of the Senate, and regardless of the senatorial rules and procedures in place."

Edward Whelan III, the president of the conservative Ethics and Public Policy Center and a former Scalia law clerk, criticized the article in a series of blog posts, in particular for addressing the wrong question. He wrote, "The immediate question before the Senate Republicans upon Justice Scalia's death was how to deal with (a) a nomination by an opposite-party president, (b) in an election year, (c) that threatens to dramatically alter the ideological composition of the Court."

Kar and Mazzone responded, "Naturally, Republican Senators would prefer to replace Justice Scalia with a Republican appointee. But does it break with over two centuries of historical tradition to turn this political preference into an attempt to divest an elected president of his constitutionally designated appointment powers, as opposed to confirming, rejecting or resisting particular candidates in ways that seek to shape and moderate a president's choice of nominees? The historical record suggests that it does."

In other words, Whelan's point that politics should take precedence over historical practice (it was okay for the Republicans to block an Obama nominee because he threatened "to dramatically alter the ideological composition of the Court") turned his political preference into an attempt to divest Obama of his power as president, as Kar and Mazzone were arguing.

When the founding fathers debated the Constitution in 1787, they returned again and again to the question of who should appoint justices of the Supreme Court. A proposal to give the president that power provoked concerns that that would give the president too much power, including perhaps some influence over the Court itself.

A proposal to give the Senate that power stirred worries that appointments would result "from cabal," as Edmund Randolph of Virginia identified potential secret deals between factions, and that with small states and large ones each represented by two senators, justices might be appointed by a minority of the people even though they were picked by a majority of states.

Nathaniel Gorham of Massachusetts proposed that the president nominate and that the Senate confirm justices. This method, he said, "had been ratified by the experience of a hundred and forty years" in his colony-turned-state. Virginia's James Madison modified the idea, recommending that the president nominate and that the nomination become an appointment within a to-be-specified number of days, unless two-thirds of the Senate opposed.

By the closing days of the constitutional convention, however, the unresolved dispute about vesting the power of appointment in the executive branch or the legislature superseded the prescient pragmatism of Madison's recommendation. The final draft of the Constitution said "The President . . . shall nominate, and by and with the Advice and Consent of the Senate, shall appoint . . . Judges of the supreme Court." The clause left to the Senate the details of how to provide advice and consent.

In the month after Scalia's death, senators from each party regularly gave speeches on the floor of the Senate to strengthen support for their party's position, with each side contending its view as a matter of constitutional principle. The legal scholar Jamal Greene of Columbia Law School argued in the *Los Angeles Times* that "past practice and practical wisdom" indicated that the Republican refusal was unconstitutional, but he went on to say that since this was the kind of "political question" federal courts do not decide, "We the people must be the judges in this case, and it will take time." Public opinion polls and news coverage filtered out these nuances. They portrayed the Republicans' refusal and the Democrats' umbrage as a political disagreement about a political appointment.

The dispute boiled down to each party insisting that it should appoint the next justice. The Democrats argued that Obama had been reelected in 2012 and that one of his duties and prerogatives under the Constitution was to nominate a justice when a seat was open on the Court. The Republicans used the political warfare about the open seat to rally their base of supporters, so a Republican would replace Obama as the next president and have the chance to fill the seat.

In March, the president nominated Chief Judge Merrick B. Garland of the US Court of Appeals for the District of Columbia Circuit. Garland seemed to be a candidate preapproved by Republicans. In 1997, Republicans had controlled the Senate with fifty-five seats. With support from thirty-two Republicans and one Democrat not voting, Garland was confirmed by 76–23 to the appeals court considered the country's second most important tribunal after the Supreme Court.

Nineteen years later, he was in his fourth year as chief judge and had served with true distinction. He had a moderate record. He held the admiration of judges across the legal spectrum on his own court. Brett Kavanaugh, a highly respected conservative judge on that bench, called Garland a "brilliant jurist" and a "good man with great integrity" who was "supremely qualified" to serve on the Supreme Court.

In *The Audacity of Hope*, Obama wrote, "If we're honest with ourselves, we'll admit that much of the time we are arguing about results—the actual decisions that the courts and the legislature make about the profound and difficult issues that help shape our lives." In that sense, he went on, "today's constitutional arguments can't be separated from politics." What distinguished the president from some liberals was his belief that there was nothing wrong with that convergence. In his book, he wrote, "I wondered if, in our reliance on the courts to vindicate not only our rights but also our values, progressives had lost too much faith in democracy."

That was part of what made Garland a strong choice for a president whose first instinct in the pursuit of justice was not to run to court: he had kept his faith. Announcing him in the Rose Garden of the White House, Obama said, "I chose a serious man and an exemplary judge, Merrick Garland. Over my seven years as president, in all my conversations with senators from both parties in which I asked their views on qualified Supreme Court nominees—this includes the previous two seats that I had to fill—the one name that has come up repeatedly, from Republicans and Democrats alike, is Merrick Garland." In 2010, when Obama picked Justice Elena Kagan for the Court, the *New York Times* reported that Garland was "the most likely alternative to Ms. Kagan and the one most likely to win easy confirmation" but that the president had "opted to save Judge Garland for when he faces a more hostile Senate and needs a nominee with more Republican support."

Obama correctly predicted the Senate's hostility but not its intensity. When Obama nominated Garland, American politics was in turmoil, more divided and discordant than at any time in two generations. With McConnell and Grassley taking the lead, both of whom voted against Garland's confirmation to the DC Circuit, the Republicans held firm in refusing to consider his nomination to the Supreme Court. The breakdown in cooperation in the Senate was so well established that there appeared to be no political cost to them. Instead, there was some benefit in the enthusiasm that their mulishness stirred among their most important supporters.

In early April, at the University of Chicago Law School, where the president had been a senior lecturer and professor of constitutional law for twelve years before he was elected to the US Senate in 2004, he met with a group of students to talk about the nomination. He said that "part of the reason I thought Merrick was ideal now is precisely because of all the polarization we were talking about earlier. What a good moment for us to have somebody who is respected by both sides, and who Chief Justice Roberts served with on the Appellate Court and befriended, and consistently said—despite being on the opposite ends of a bunch of decisions—said this is somebody who, if he says you're wrong, you've got to think long and hard about it. He embodies and models what it is that we want to see in our jurisprudence."

The president had also said this about polarization:

I think what's important for all of you to understand—because you're going to be not just lawyers appearing in court, potentially, but custodians of our legal system and our democracy—is if you start getting into a situation in which the process of appointing judges is so broken, so partisan that an eminently qualified jurist cannot even get a hearing, then we are going to see the kinds of sharp, partisan polarization that has come to characterize our electoral politics seeping entirely into the judicial system. And the courts will be just an extension of our legislatures and our elections and our politics.

Law and Politics

A large body of scholarship, by political scientists and legal scholars, has sought to measure the extent of the Supreme Court's independence as an institution and of justices as individuals. There is a surprisingly wide consensus that, with prominent exceptions, the Court has maintained its independence in part by limiting its exercise of independence. It rarely gets ahead of public opinion, the consensus holds. When it is judging whether there is a basis for striking down a law and, as a result, changing a controversial matter of public policy, it often explicitly addresses public opinion by counting the number of states that have already made that change. "The limits of judicial independence are those imposed by the polity," the scholar Tom S. Clark has written. "Judicial discretion exists to the extent there is sufficient public support for judicial independence."

That public support, or lack of it, is sometimes expressed through Congress. Court-curbing measures, as Clark calls legislative attacks—cutbacks in the jurisdiction of the Supreme Court and lower federal courts, rejections of new judgeships, long delays in confirming nominees for judgeships—reflect Congress's view of the Court and other federal courts, or the view of the majority party in the House of Representatives and the Senate. This support does not require agreement: it is common for critics of Court rulings, for example, to accept them because the rulings are seen as the results of fair deliberation.

The most controversial limitation on judicial independence—and on impartial judicial opinions—is personal preference, the combination of perspectives that a justice brings to the job as a result of his or her prior experiences. Among political scientists, the "attitudinal model," as it is called, held sway for decades. Leading practitioners of it, the political scientists Jeffrey Segal and Harold Spaeth, concluded from their research that justices make policy and that they do so based on their personal preferences about policy, sometimes exclusively and otherwise primarily. As Lee Epstein and Jack Knight of Washington University summarized this view about the work of justices, "rules based on precedent" are "nothing more than smokescreens" behind which they hide their values.

Segal and Spaeth disparaged what they called the legal model—the idea that legal rules and principles guide justices to the one right result when they apply the law to the facts in a case—as illogical and unsupported by the history of the Court. The model puts great stock in legal precedent—for example, rules and principles established by past Court decisions that bind the Court to apply them in similar cases and maintain the stability of the law. But justices often disagree about the meaning of precedents and have ready tools of legal logic for getting around them or limiting them, so the precedents are not binding on the Court.

The most persuasive evidence about the utility of the attitudinal model has been empirical scholarship supporting it. Studies have documented the ideological differences among justices and how those differences have been more accurate predictors of how justices vote in cases than their judicial philosophies, with a lot of consistency in the voting patterns of justices with similar ideologies and of individual justices over time and across different areas of law.

There is a more recent body of empirical work testing hypotheses about the roles of law and politics in shaping judicial decisions, which the legal scholars Thomas J. Miles and Cass R. Sunstein call the "New Legal Realism." They note that instead of treating law and politics as competing influences, this recent scholarship recognizes that both can be influences: "A distinguishing feature of the New Legal Realism is the close examination of reported cases in order to understand how judicial personality, understood in various ways, influences legal outcomes, and how legal institutions constrain or unleash these influences."

This scholarship addresses important realities that the attitudinal model does not. The Supreme Court, even in years defined by steely disagreement in major cases, regularly decides a high percentage of cases unanimously. In the 2015 term, the Court decided 44 percent of its cases unanimously. The term before, it was 40 percent, and the term before that, 66 percent—two out of every three cases.

Those figures do not tell the whole story. SCOTUSblog, in its annual presentation of statistics about the completed term, distinguishes among levels of agreement. The most significant comes when justices agree on the outcome and the opinion explaining it, without any reservations expressed through concurring opinions.

Then there are cases where a justice, or more than one, agrees about the outcome but joins only part of the majority opinion, either declining to join another part or writing a separate opinion to present an individual position. Finally, the thinnest kind of agreement comes when justices agree about the outcome and nothing else, so each justice can write a separate opinion that conflicts with the reasoning in the opinion of another justice. In the 2015 term, the percentages of those types of agreement were, respectively, 29 percent, 7 percent, and 8 percent—with the agreement in about one-third of the cases, 15 percent out of 44 percent, only partial.

And there is still more that those figures do not tell. In the 2013 term, for example, while the Court was unanimous in two out of every three cases, and it had the most significant yet narrowest kind of agreement in almost two out of every five cases, that said nothing about whether the agreement came in a broad ruling or in a narrow one. That term, the Court's sometimes deep ideological divisions were masked by many very narrow outcomes in cases.

A well-known study done in 1986 by the political scientist Jon Gottschall compared the records of fifty-five appeals-court appointees of the conservative Reagan administration with the records of the fifty-six appointees of the liberal Carter Administration. Reagan and Carter judges on the regional US courts of appeals agreed 74 percent of the time. But in the other 26 percent, judges appointed by Carter voted for a liberal outcome in 95 percent of the cases, while judges appointed by Reagan voted that way in just 5 percent.

In cases where they agreed, it is likely that the law compelled it. Because the US courts of appeals have little discretion about their docket and, in many cases, are functioning as courts of errors, correcting misapplications of law to fact by trial courts, panels of judges on those courts agree a high percentage of a time—around 80 percent. In the whole of the twentieth century, they reversed only about 30 percent of cases they heard. The Supreme Court, on the other hand, has almost total discretion about its docket, so the percentage of unanimous cases is notably lower than for appeals courts. In the twentieth century, the Court reversed about 60 percent of the cases it heard. The Court often takes hard cases where there is a large disagreement among the regional courts of appeals or a constitutional question that should be answered.

The size of the Court's docket now seems to reflect its difficulty: the smaller it is, the harder the cases. During the nineteenth century, the Court decided all cases appealed to it when it had jurisdiction. The regional courts of appeals were established in 1891 to share some of the caseload when the Supreme Court was struggling to handle it. When that happened again a generation later, Congress passed the Judiciary Act of 1925. The statute relieved the Court of much, but not all, of its entire mandatory docket.

In 1988, with the full support of all nine justices, who wrote a letter to Congress saying that mandatory cases were taking too much of the Court's time, Congress passed the Supreme Court Case Selection Act. It relieved the Court of almost all its remaining mandatory cases—under the few federal statutes calling for mandatory review, like the Insecticide, Fungicide, and Rodenticide Act, and in certain categories, like when a federal court held a federal or state statute unconstitutional or when a state court heard a challenge under federal law and held a federal or state law invalid. The Court is still required to hear appeals in elections cases, reapportionment cases, and a few others.

When the 1988 Act went into effect, the docket began to fall, from 165 cases in 1988 to 145 in '89 to 123 in '90, down to the current average of about 80 a term. But a host of other factors are influential, including the preferences of justices. In his thirty-one years on the Court beginning in 1962, Justice Byron R. White believed strongly that the Court should resolve as many differences of outlook among courts of appeals as possible—even slight conflicts. Between 1986 and 1992, for example, he voted to grant review an average of 216 times a term, 67 percent more than the second-place justice in that period. White, all by himself, because he was often as persuasive about this preference as he was invested in it, was likely responsible for the Court hearing 28 extra cases each term, or close to one-fifth of its cases.

On the other hand, the legal scholars Margaret Meriwether Cordray and Richard Cordray documented that, in the decade from the mid-1980s to the mid-'90s, the replacement of five justices had a considerable effect on the size of the docket, with the arrival of Justices Kennedy and Scalia having the largest impact. The Cordrays wrote that they "settled into abnegating roles in the discretionary review process, voting to grant review less often than any other Justice."

The scholars Ryan J. Owens and David A. Simon have found, in addition, that ideology has played a significant role in determining the size of the Court's docket, just as it has in on related matters: which cases the Court decides to hear, the justice to whom the chief justice or the senior justice in the majority asks to write the majority opinion, the extent to which justices bargain about the content of opinions, and so on. They write, "Justices who agree ideologically with opinion authors seek changes in their opinions only 15 percent of the time. Ideological opponents of that author, however, seek changes to that same opinion nearly 57 percent of the time." Through statistical analysis assessing how ideology (as opposed to the passage of the 1988 Act and other factors) affected the size of the Court's docket between the 1940 and 2008 terms, they concluded: "The Court decides more cases when it is ideologically cohesive and fewer cases when it is ideologically fractured." The low number of cases in recent terms reflects the fissures on the current Court.

When Richard M. Nixon campaigned for president in 1968, he made the Supreme Court a major issue. One of Nixon's main TV ads portrayed the country as out of control, with crime on the rise. The Republican Party platform promised law and order in place of lawlessness, which Nixon blamed in part on Court decisions providing constitutional safeguards to criminal defendants at the expense of public safety.

Nixon practiced dog-whistle politics, as Michael Graetz and Linda Greenhouse recounted in *The Burger Court and the Rise of the Judicial Right*. He told a Southern audience: "I think some of our judges have gone too far in assuming unto themselves a mandate which is not there, and that is to put their social and economic ideas into their decisions." He linked crime with race and race with judges who had gone too far. He pledged to appoint "strict constructionists" who would tighten up criminal law in particular.

In his first term as president, Nixon got the opportunity to appoint four justices: Warren E. Burger as chief justice in 1969, Harry A. Blackmun in 1970, and Lewis F. Powell Jr. and William H. Rehnquist in 1972. Burger was chief until 1986. From 1972 through 1975, he presided over a Court with three liberals and six moderates and conservatives who often yielded a majority of five. From 1975 until he retired, Burger presided over a Court with two liberals and seven other justices who often yielded a majority of five.

A prevailing view of the Burger Court is that as a result of the influence of moderate justices—Potter Stewart, Byron White, John Paul Stevens, and Sandra Day O'Connor—it did not reverse the direction of Supreme Court law in the Warren era. The legal scholar Vincent Blasi called this period "the counter-revolution that wasn't." Compared with the conservative expectations and liberal anxieties that Nixon raised, there was no counterrevolution.

But as Graetz and Greenhouse have showed, the Burger Court began to move Supreme Court law to the right in prominent areas—with some significant exceptions. Two of the most profound shifts took place in civil rights and criminal justice. After *Brown v. Board of Education*, two cases typically vie for the second most important civil rights case dealing with public schools: 1973's *San Antonio Independent School District v. Rodriguez* and *Milliken v. Bradley* from the following year. Both addressed the issue of remedies for inadequate schools and, by 5–4 votes, rejected *Brown*'s deep commitment to equality.

The first, brought by mostly Mexican American parents from a poor school district in Texas, concerned the large discrepancy between the funding for and quality of public schools in poor and rich districts in the state, because of its reliance on local property taxes for about half the funding for public education. Spending per student by the poor district (it was 90 percent Mexican American, 6 percent black, 4 percent white) was three-fifths the amount of spending by the rich one (81 percent white, 18 percent Mexican American, 1 percent black): the property tax rate in the poor district was 24 percent higher, but the average value of property per student was 88 percent lower.

A special three-judge panel of federal judges found the Texas system of public school financing unconstitutional under the Fourteenth Amendment's Equal Protection Clause. Relying on *Brown* ("Today, education is perhaps the most important function of state and local governments."), the court found that education was a fundamental right under the federal Constitution and that the state's education funding system, organized by school district, was unacceptable because that was the same as organizing the system by differences of wealth. The court ordered Texas to change its system so that the amount spent on a child's education did not depend on the wealth of his or her neighborhood.

With Powell writing for the majority, the Court rejected the lower court's key holdings about education as a fundamental right and about a district's wealth as an unacceptable means of organizing the funding system. It found that the system provided every student with public education while fostering local involvement through local determination of tax rates and quality of education. The forty-nine other states used the same system, so the ruling "momentously influenced the future of public education in America," Graetz and Greenhouse write. "*Rodriguez* guaranteed that the resources of public schools would remain grossly unequal throughout the land," unless a ruling in a state court prohibited that in a state. The Supreme Court ruling "eviscerated the most promising alternative avenue for claims based on racial discrimination."

In *Milliken v. Bradley*, a majority opinion by Burger rejected the remedy of busing students across the line between a segregated urban school district and a suburban district that was not segregated. After extensive testimony, Federal District Judge Stephen Roth from Detroit had found that the school board segregated the city's schools. The board did that, he said, by where it located schools and by how it drew school boundaries and attendance zones, among other ways.

He also found that policies of the state of Michigan contributed to the segregation. Nearly all the students in Detroit schools were black. Nearly all the surrounding suburban students were white. Roth ordered that the Detroit school district consolidate with some suburban districts and that they bus students between city and suburban schools. The US Court of Appeals for the Sixth Circuit upheld the order.

The gist of the Supreme Court's decision overturning the lower-court rulings was that the remedy to address Detroit's segregation had to match the extent of the violation to the Constitution. In dissent, Thurgood Marshall wrote, "Today's holding, I fear, is more a reflection of a perceived public mood that we have gone far enough in enforcing the Constitution's guarantee of equal justice than it is the product of neutral principles of law." Coming only twenty years after *Brown*, the decision in the Detroit case marked the end of the surprisingly brief period in which the Court, appealing to basic principles of fairness, promoted integrated schools.

Graetz and Greenhouse write, "No one can deny that, in combination with *Rodriguez*, the Burger Court's decision in *Milliken* doomed to failure the Warren Court's effort to ensure integrated schools of equal quality."

The Court expressed the depth of its equivocation about education and race in 1978, in *Regents of the University of California v. Bakke*. There, by 5–4, with Powell writing for the majority, the Court found that racial quotas could not be used in university admissions because racial and ethnic classifications were inherently suspect. As his biographer John C. Jeffries Jr. has explained, Powell wanted to preserve "for the future the ideal of a color-blind society."

But, Jeffries continued, Powell believed that giving preference in admissions to well-qualified members of racial and ethnic minorities was "vital to an integrated society" and that outlawing the practice would be, in Powell's words, "a disaster for the country." So Powell voted with the four justices who believed that a plan to set aside sixteen seats for minority students in a hundred-person medical-school class at the University of California at Davis would be a form of reverse discrimination. But he also voted with the other four justices, who thought that the set-aside program was a necessary and constitutional response to the nation's history of racial discrimination.

Powell's approach led to the conclusion that there was no difference between positive discrimination designed to include a group and negative discrimination designed to exclude one. The Court required that an affirmative action program in education prove that it serves a compelling interest (educational diversity meets that standard) and, in addition, that it is carefully tailored to serve that purpose—giving a preference for racial and ethnic minorities but not a guaranteed place.

This requirement led to a preoccupation with how the remedy of affirmative action could be justified, as opposed to why it was needed. In dissent in the *Bakke* case, Justice Thurgood Marshall addressed the consequences of that shift. "I fear that we have come full circle," he concluded. "After the Civil War our Government started several 'affirmative action' programs," he wrote. Referring to landmark rulings in which the Supreme Court cut off Congress's efforts to promote racial equality and then upheld the rule of separate but equal treatment for blacks, he went on: "This Court in the *Civil Rights Cases* and *Plessy* v. *Ferguson* destroyed the movement toward complete equality. For almost a century no action was taken, and this non-action was with the tacit approval of the courts. Then we had *Brown* v. *Board of Education* and the Civil Rights Acts of Congress, followed by numerous affirmative-action programs. *Now,* we have this Court again stepping in, this time to stop affirmative-action programs of the type used by the University of California."

In criminal justice, the Warren Court established and extended rules for police to follow: the ban on unreasonable searches and seizures under the Fourth Amendment, the privilege against self-incrimination under the

Fifth Amendment, and the guarantee of legal counsel for criminal defendants who could be jailed or imprisoned if convicted. The Burger Court retained these rights and, in some cases, strengthened them.

But as Harvard Law School's Carol Steiker has explained, while the Court maintained these rules of conduct, reassuring the public about the judiciary's commitment to these basic constitutional rights, it significantly cut back on the consequences when police violate those rights—rules of decision that courts must use to enforce the law. The Burger Court made dog-whistle rulings, Steiker holds, with the public hearing the reassuring message about the affirmation of constitutional rights, while police heard the consequential message that for some violations of those rights, there is no penalty because, for example, the violation is judged harmless. There was no counterrevolution about rights for criminal defendants, Steiker writes, but there was a "counter-revolutionary war against the Warren Court's constitutional 'remedies.'"

Under landmark rulings of that Court, a key result was the exclusion of evidence obtained in violation of a constitutional right; this so-called exclusionary rule went on to become a staple of cop shows on TV. Steiker calls the result of some Burger Court decisions "inclusionary rules"—"radical" narrowings of Warren Court holdings that "permit the use at trial of admittedly unconstitutionally obtained evidence or that let stand criminal convictions based on such evidence." The result was a considerable shift in the law concerning criminal justice. The Supreme Court did what Nixon said he was aiming for in his four appointments of justices: the Court became, Steiker writes, "less sympathetic to claims of individual rights and more accommodating to assertions of the need for public order."

One of the most startling cutbacks was to the right to counsel in criminal cases. "Lawyers in criminal court courts are necessities, not luxuries," Justice Hugo Black wrote for a unanimous Warren Court when it established that right. But the Burger Court said, in effect, that while a criminal defendant faced with the prospect of time behind bars had a right to legal representation, the counsel he was entitled to need not be competent.

The Court held that the "benchmark for judging any claim of ineffectiveness must be whether counsel's conduct so undermined the proper functioning of the adversarial process that the trial cannot be relied on as having produced a just result." As Graetz and Greenhouse write, "The case is among the most cited in Supreme Court history, having been relied on by federal and state courts in thousands of cases, making it extremely rare for a court to overturn a conviction or a sentence because counsel was ineffective."

The Rehnquist Court continued to maintain constitutional rights for criminal defendants while hollowing out remedies for them in an almost continual march of retrenchment. But with Rehnquist's ascension to be chief justice, Antonin Scalia's appointment to fill Rehnquist's seat, and Clarence Thomas's replacement of Thurgood Marshall, by 1991 the Court was considerably more conservative than it had been under Burger. With Sandra Day O'Connor and Anthony Kennedy, there was a conservative majority of five that brought about what the legal scholars Jack Balkin and Sanford Levinson have called "a fundamental shift in constitutional thought and constitutional doctrine." Federalism was one area where that happened—the relationship between the federal and state governments.

The new conservative majority ruled that states violating certain federal rights were immune from federal court judgments ordering them to pay money to compensate victims of those violations when the federal statute authorizing those lawsuits was based on the power under the Constitution to regulate commerce. They extended that logic to state court judgments, saying that private parties could not sue states for violations of the same federal laws there either: that would be an affront to their dignity.

The same five limited the power of Congress to pass civil rights legislation to remedy or prevent violations as the Court interpreted them, only if they were "congruent and proportional" to the injury being remedied or prevented. The conservative majority extended this logic to patents when it struck down laws making a state liable for the intentional infringement of patents, to women who were victims of rape and related violence when it struck down a law allowing them to sue the people who attacked them, to people who were victims of age discrimination when it struck down a law allowing state employees to sue the state they worked for, and, eventually, to people who were victims of discrimination because of a disability by holding that states were immune from lawsuits under the act. Balkin and Levenson observed that this was part of a "transformation in constitutional doctrine," which involved "a fairly consistent application of a core set of ideological premises"—limits on federal power, promotion of states' rights, and very narrow construction of federal civil rights laws, among other emphases.

As Dawn E. Johnsen, a professor of law at Indiana University, explained, these ideas do not appear in the Constitution. Instead, the conservative majority derived them from its understanding of the authority of states because of their sovereignty and because of the power of the Supreme Court over Congress through judicial supremacy. Only the judiciary could define the substantive scope of the provisions of the Fourteenth Amendment, the Court said. Even when it recognized a right that Congress sought to protect, it was vigilant in scrutinizing how Congress was carrying that out.

Article I, Section 1 of the Constitution begins, "All legislative powers herein granted shall be vested in a Congress of the United States." The upshot of the Rehnquist conservative majority was a notable limitation on the power of Congress under America's fundamental law. "The end result," Johnsen wrote, was "a judiciary with expanded, self-proclaimed authority to say what the Constitution means, and a Congress significantly diminished in its ability to set national policy, to protect important rights and interests, and to participate in the process of constitutional interpretation."

As Johnsen suggested, the Rehnquist Court made dog-whistle rulings in transforming the workings of the structure of the American constitutional system. For the public, the message was a modest one about national authority under the Constitution: the Court was restoring balance in the federal system by respecting the sovereign power of the states. Even for well-informed Court-watchers, its federalism initiative was shrouded in the notions of state sovereign immunity and of congruence and proportionality of legislation.

Judge John T. Noonan Jr.—a senior member of the US Court of Appeals for the Ninth Circuit and a philosopher, theologian, and historian before Ronald Reagan appointed him to the bench in 1985—attacked the basis for and logic of this federalism in his 2003 book *Narrowing the Nation's Power*. "The results are incomprehensible without an understanding of the legal doctrines on which they are based," he wrote. "The doctrines are abstract. Abstractness gives them an appearance of depth they do not deserve." In his view, the Court's use of the concept of state sovereign immunity improperly interfered with the power of Congress to enact protections for Americans on a national scale.

These changes represented a success for the Reagan administration. During his first inaugural address, Ronald Reagan pledged, "It is my intention to curb the size and influence of the Federal establishment and to demand recognition of the distinction between the powers granted to the federal government and those reserved to the states or the people. All of us need to be reminded that the federal government did not create the states; the states created the federal government."

Reagan did not succeed in fulfilling all those ambitions: rather than curb the size of the federal government, his administration took on more new debt than all the preceding administrations in American history combined; and the civilian federal workforce grew during his presidency. But the Reagan administration was remarkably successful in getting big parts of its vision of the constitutional system adopted by the Supreme Court.

The Justice Department issued a series of reports—like *Guidelines on Constitutional Litigation*, 1988, and *The Constitution in the Year 2000: Choices Ahead in Constitutional Interpretation*, 1988—laying out the conservative Reagan vision.

Among the fifteen issues it reported on was: "Will the Tenth Amendment"—saying that any power that the Constitution does not grant to the federal government is reserved to the states or to the American people—"play a significant role in protecting the states from federal control?"

In most of the 5–4 rulings that restricted the power of Congress and strengthened the sovereignty of states, the majority included three justices Reagan appointed (O'Connor, Scalia, and Kennedy) and one he elevated (Rehnquist), with the fifth vote supplied by a justice George H. W. Bush appointed (Thomas). Major changes in the law of federalism came after Reagan left office, but they followed the Reagan administration blueprint. They resulted from the administration's emphasis on ideology as an essential criterion for federal judicial appointees, especially to the Supreme Court.

The Rehnquist Court's 2000 ruling by 5–4 in *Bush v. Gore* was "not dictated by the law in any sense," the University of Chicago's David A. Strauss later wrote: the five conservatives flouted judicial restraint and states' rights by stopping the Florida Supreme Court from interpreting Florida law and halting the recount of the presidential election before it was finished. After determining that George W. Bush would be elected president, they declared their handiwork a nonprecedent ("Our consideration is limited to the present circumstances"). That outcome led to the Roberts Court.

When George W. Bush appointed Samuel Alito to replace Sandra Day O'Connor, the Supreme Court immediately shifted further to the right. O'Connor had been a member of the Rehnquist Court's federalism five, but she was a moderate member of that Court. Alito was a movement conservative, as the Reagan administration called its young lawyers. At a discussion held by the Center for American Progress, William Yeomans of American University's Washington College of Law, speaking ironically, described Alito's jurisprudence as pragmatic and flexible—sometimes originalist or strict constructionist, other times solicitous of corporate or individual rights, especially when the individuals were Christians and whites. This approach allowed him to use doctrines as necessary to arrive at a set of ideologically driven conclusions reflecting the conservative legal agenda.

Yeomans focused on Alito favoring restrictions to the exclusionary rule and defendants' rights more generally, opposing privacy and the right of women to choose having an abortion, opposing affirmative action in particular and race-consciousness in government programs in general, supporting a restrictive reading of the commerce power, favoring a skeptical review of federal regulation, and enthusing about expansion of gun rights, among other positions.

By some measures, Rehnquist was the most conservative member of the Court since 1937. But in 5–4 cases where the split was based on ideology, Roberts was the fourth most conservative justice between 1937 and 2012—and only the twenty-second most conservative in cases where there were three or fewer dissenting votes. As Lee Epstein, William Landes, and Richard Posner, who did the study leading to these conclusions, wrote about the chief justice, "He is a reliable conservative in the most closely contested cases but moderate when his vote can't change the outcome. This is consistent with a Chief Justice's interest in being on the winning side in most cases; otherwise it looks as if he can't control his Court."

Roberts's vote with the Court's liberals in June of 2012 to uphold most of the Affordable Care Act was a momentous exception to his usual conservative voting, but on the ground that it was authorized under Congress's power to levy taxes and was not valid under the Constitution's Commerce Clause. Some commentators saw in Roberts's vote his concern for the legitimacy of the Court, which would have been trashed if it had intervened in such an intensely political issue and, in the extreme opposite of judicial restraint, overturned the act. But in Roberts's opinion in the case, some also saw a sly and sinister expansion of conservative doctrine on the question of what sort of laws violate the Commerce Clause, which might be invoked in the future to strike down statutes passed to protect the general welfare.

In 5–4 cases with an ideological split, the addition of Roberts and Alito generally made the Court more conservative than it had been under Rehnquist for the first five terms of the Roberts Court, from 2005 until 2010. With that Court's decisions plotted on a graph, there was a notable uptick in liberal outcomes from the 2012 through the 2014 terms, with the percentage of liberal outcomes as high in the 2014 term as in the 1957 term of the liberal Warren Court. But the level of agreement on the Roberts Court in those cases was generally very thin. Thomas Moylan Keck of Syracuse University observed, "The Roberts Court is striking down statutes less often than the Rehnquist Court did, but when it does, it's willing to swing for the fences"—mainly to the right, but occasionally to the left as well.

The signature ruling of the Roberts Court until the death of Antonin Scalia was the 5–4 decision in 2010 in *Citizens United v. Federal Election Commission*, where the conservative majority ruled that money equals speech and that placing limits on the independent spending of corporations, unions, and other organizations in political campaigns would infringe on their right to free speech under the First Amendment. The Court overturned two precedents in reaching that conclusion—one only seven years old, the other twenty.

The case was the product of a longtime legal campaign led by James Bopp Jr., a Republican lawyer in Terre Haute, Indiana. He was general counsel for the National Right to Life organization when the Federal Election Commission tried to block it in 1980 from distributing voter guides before the national election about candidates' positions on abortion rights and other social issues. Bopp sued and won. His premise was that politics is improved when there is more money being spent on it, because more money means more information and, in particular, more individualized messages for segments of voters. He was convinced that sitting politicians try to restrict money in politics to protect their own seats.

Still, the conservatives on the Roberts Court made the broad ruling they did in Bopp's case on their own initiative. A group called Citizens United made a ninety-minute campaign film attacking Hillary Clinton as a candidate for president in 2008. A federal district court ruled that the main federal law regulating campaign finance applied to the film as "a broadcast communication," so corporate funds could not pay $1.2 million to a cable operator to let subscribers stream the film for free. The questions for the Supreme Court were: Did the statute's curb on broadcasts funded by corporations apply to video on demand? Did an exemption for some nonprofits from the statute's rule limiting corporate spending cover ideological nonprofits like the group called Citizens United, which produced the film? Rather than address those questions about the meaning of the statute, however, the Court decided to address whether, to prevent corruption in politics, the Constitution allows limits on independent spending by corporations and other organizations.

In one of the two oral arguments about the case before the Supreme Court, former Clinton Solicitor General Seth P. Waxman said that if the Court wanted to reconsider its longtime law that corporate spending in politics should be regulated to avoid corruption or the appearance of it, "it should do so in a case in which those interests are forthrightly challenged with a proper and full record" gathered in a trial.

Chief Justice Roberts responded as if Waxman, one of the most esteemed appellate advocates in the country, had made a naïve—even uninformed—suggestion: "Well, Mr. Waxman, the government did have that opportunity, and the government compiled a record," and "yet we hear nothing about what the record showed." Waxman replied that that was because the issues pressed by Citizens United during the trial "did nothing whatsoever to implicate the foundation" of the precedents the Court seemed to be considering overturning. He went on, "And all I'm saying is, if you want to re-examine the predicates, the existence and magnitude of interests that Congress has" protected for more than a century, the Court should do that in a case "where the issue is squarely presented." The plea fell on deaf ears.

Citizens United represents judicial activism in the service of judicial supremacy of an extreme kind—swinging for the fences: instead of answering whether the federal statute applied to the broadcast of the film attacking Hillary Clinton, the Court's five conservatives reached the constitutional issue they wanted to, upending a well-established principle of election law and unleashing a huge new cascade of so-called independent expenditures by corporations in American politics. For a conservative majority seen as the protector of the moneyed class in American life, politics seemed to propel the ruling in which politics and law were indistinguishable.

It is common to yoke *Citizens United*'s protection of the moneyed class in public life with a series of decisions the Roberts Court has made protecting that class in the marketplace by upholding (under the Federal Arbitration Act) clauses in contracts written by corporations that require their employees or customers to pursue any grievances they have in private arbitration rather than a public court. They are usually presented as anti-class-action cases because mandatory arbitration clauses avoid those cases. They also often avoid many private arbitration challenges, because the cost to an individual to bring one is more than he would get if he won his challenge.

But one in this line of cases, *American Express v. Italian Colors* (2013), was an antitrust case, making it easier to see the broader political, economic, and social importance of this area of law. A group of merchants could not bring a class action against the company even on antitrust grounds because each had signed a contract that required complaints to be taken to individual arbitration. American Express required merchants who wanted to accept its corporate and premium charge cards to accept, as well, basic American Express credit cards at a fee 30 percent higher than the fees of other credit cards.

The merchants sought damages of about five thousand dollars, but it would cost each merchant hundreds of thousands of dollars to try to prove an antitrust claim. The arbitration provision in their contracts kept them from sharing the cost or from consolidating their claims into one case, so each was left with no way to press a claim. Italian Colors Restaurant and others argued that, by using its power in the market for the corporate and premium cards to require them to accept the third card and its higher costs, the company was subjecting them to a "tying arrangement" in violation of federal antitrust law. The merchants argued that the arbitration clause meant that despite the strength of their claims under this law, they could not bring them: they argued that for that reason, they should be allowed to proceed as a group. The Supreme Court, by 5–3, ruled that the merchants could not bring a class action against the company even on antitrust grounds: each had signed a contract that required them to bring complaints through individual arbitration.

The University of Texas Law School's Joseph Fishkin and William E. Forbath, in part of their work in progress titled *The Constitution of Opportunity*, write, "What drives the Court's view of arbitration and the FAA [the Federal

Arbitration Act] in the end, is not a deeply considered understanding of congressional intent but a deeply rooted view about the place of private contract ordering in relation to public law." It should have seen that the merchants were challenging a monopolist's use of its market power to get around antimonopoly law. Instead, the conservative majority did not see the monopoly or pretended not to, treating American Express and each merchant as equal parties who had willingly entered into the contract with the arbitration clause, rather than as unequals with the finance company dictating the terms.

In another important study, Epstein, Landes, and Posner analyzed about two thousand Supreme Court decisions from 1946 to 2011. They found that the five conservatives of the Roberts Court until Scalia's death were among the top ten of the thirty-six justices who served in that period. The two justices in those sixty-five years most likely to vote in favor of business interests were Alito and Roberts. No justice appointed by a Republican was less favorable to business than any justice appointed by a Democrat. The Roberts Court, by the numbers, was the most probusiness Court since World War II—and, by the reckoning of Court-watchers, the most probusiness since the pre-1937 Court during the Great Depression.

The major Roberts Court rulings upholding the heart of the Affordable Care Act, being in favor of federal benefits for same-sex partners, and finding a constitutional right to same-sex marriage reached liberal results—and they were very significant. But in the Roberts Court's first ten years, ending before the 2015 term, there were scores of conservative decisions curbing voting rights, abortion rights, union rights, criminal defendants' rights, access to courts, affirmative action, and many other individual interests and rights. Before that term, depending on the docket, the Roberts Court had strongly reinforced, deeply extended, or largely maintained the Court's character as a conservative institution over almost five decades.

C h a p t e r 4

October Term 2015

The most important ruling of the 2015 term was about abortion rights. By 5–3 in a case called *Whole Woman's Health v. Hellerstedt*, on the last day of the term, the Supreme Court struck down two provisions of a Texas statute that made it much more difficult for many women to have an abortion. Without any medical benefits for them from these so-called health-and-safety provisions, the statute was a TRAP law—Targeted Regulation of Abortion Providers—intended to impede them. The vote of Justice Antonin Scalia likely would have made the case a typical 5–4 term-ending clash between conservatives and liberals but likely would not have changed the result.

Anthony M. Kennedy, not long before his eightieth birthday, cast the critical vote. As the most senior of the justices in the majority, measured by years on the Court, he had the prerogative of assigning the Court's opinion. Based on his practice in recent terms, the odds were good that he would write it himself. Instead, he chose Stephen G. Breyer to write it. Breyer wrote a crisp, quietly stern opinion, which was the Court's most important statement about abortion rights in twenty-four years.

Abortion has been among the most divisive of the wedge issues in American politics and constitutional law for two generations. The Texas case tested the Court's tolerance for laws that claimed to have one purpose when they clearly had another—by saying their goal was to protect women's health when it was really to protect, as unborn life, the fetuses that pregnant women carried.

A key question about the test was how the Court would apply the legal standard of that generation-old case, *Planned Parenthood v. Casey*: Would it retain the standard's respect for a woman's right to choose an abortion or carry her pregnancy to term, along with its deference to a state that wanted to protect life throughout a pregnancy? Or would it let Texas's antiabortion politics further change American law by restricting the Court's protection of a woman's right to choose and the dignity that represents? It was a clear example of how the Republican Court's rightward shift affected even its best-known liberal holding— that the Constitution protects a woman's right to choose.

In 1992, the controlling opinion began, "Liberty finds no refuge in a jurisprudence of doubt. Yet 19 years after our holding that the Constitution protects a woman's right to terminate her pregnancy in its early stages, that definition of liberty is still questioned. Joining the respondents as *amicus curiae*, the United States, as it has done in five other cases in the last decade, again asks us to overrule *Roe*."

With the replacement of the liberal Thurgood Marshall by the conservative Clarence Thomas at the beginning of the 1991–92 term, it had seemed quite possible that the Court led by the conservative Chief Justice William H. Rehnquist would overturn *Roe v. Wade* and declare that there was no constitutional right for a woman to choose an abortion. The papers of Justice Harry A. Blackmun showed that Rehnquist drafted an opinion for the *Casey* case that would have overturned *Roe*.

Instead, Kennedy joined Justices Sandra Day O'Connor and David Souter to make a moderate plurality of three. Out of respect for *stare decisis*—standing by a decision made—they reaffirmed "the essential holding" in *Roe v. Wade*: women retained the constitutional right to choose. With abortion, they wrote, "the liberty of the woman is at stake in a sense unique to the human condition and so unique to the law."

But the justices employed a different way of analyzing statutes regulating abortion. They replaced the strict scrutiny that *Roe* had required courts to use, which strongly protected the right to choose by requiring a state to meet a high and skeptical standard in justifying any abortion-related regulation, with a test about "undue burden"— a legal restriction with "the purpose or effect of placing a substantial obstacle in the path of a woman seeking an abortion of a nonviable fetus." Breyer's 2016 opinion clarified that test by focusing on how to calibrate the effect. He introduced a balancing of burdens and benefits. The rule announced in *Casey*, he explained, "requires that courts consider the burdens a law imposes on abortion access together with the benefits" that the law confers.

One of the Texas provisions was what he called an admitting-privileges requirement, the other a surgical-center requirement. The first was that a doctor performing or inducing an abortion must have admitting privileges at a hospital within thirty miles. The second was that an "abortion facility" must meet the "minimum standards" for ambulatory surgical centers under Texas law—specifications about the size of the nursing staff, the dimensions of the building, and other requirements, like a preoperation holding room, a postop recovery suite, and high standards for heating, ventilation, and air conditioning.

Neither of the requirements conferred any benefit, Breyer wrote. Doctors providing abortions were already required to have admitting privileges at a local hospital or a working arrangement with a doctor who did, "to ensure the necessary back up for medical complications." And, as the factual record in the case showed, "abortion in Texas was extremely safe with particularly low rates of serious complications and virtually no deaths occurring on account of the procedure." Breyer noted, "We add that, when directly asked at oral argument whether Texas knew of a single instance in which the new requirement would have helped even one woman obtain better treatment, Texas admitted that there was no evidence in the record of such a case."

In addition, the factual record showed, ambulatory surgical centers would not significantly lower the risks of abortion, which were already very low. Between 2001 and 2012 in Texas, five deaths occurred as a result of abortions—"or about one every two years," Breyer wrote. The risk of death during childbirth nationally was 14 times as great, and "the mortality rate for liposuction, another outpatient procedure," was "28 times higher than the mortality rate for abortion."

Breyer went on, "The record makes clear that the surgical-center requirement provides no benefit when complications arise in the context of an abortion produced through medication. That is because, in such a case, complications would almost always arise only after the patient has left the facility."

He concluded, "The upshot is that this record evidence, along with the absence of any evidence to the contrary, provides ample support for the District Court's conclusion that '[m]any of the building standards mandated by the act and its implementing rules have such a tangential relationship to patient safety in the context of abortion as to be nearly arbitrary.'"

On the other hand, the record was full of evidence about substantial burdens. The rate of abortion in Texas in the years leading up to the lawsuit, Breyer said, had been about 15 to 16 percent of reported pregnancies, for a total number of between 60,000 and 72,000 abortions a year. When Texas began to enforce the admitting-privileges requirement, the number of clinics in the state providing abortions was cut in half, from about forty to about twenty.

If the surgical-requirement provision went into effect, the number would likely fall to seven or perhaps eight facilities in Houston, Dallas/Fort Worth, Austin, and San Antonio, and it was very unlikely they could handle the demand. In addition, the number of women of childbearing age living more than 50 miles from a clinic would increase by 150 percent; more than 100 miles, by 325 percent; more than 150 miles, by 1,047 percent; and more than 200 miles, by 7,500 percent.

Breyer concluded, "In the face of no threat to women's health, Texas seeks to force women to travel long distances to get abortions in crammed-to-capacity superfacilities. Patients seeking these services are less likely to get the kind of individualized attention, serious conversation, and emotional support that doctors at less taxed facilities may have offered." All this was likely to be "harmful to, not supportive of, women's health."

The abortion ruling was widely greeted as a landmark and as strong evidence of a turn to the left by the Court. That's how political science coded it, because the ruling protected the right of abortion from the state law provisions. It was perhaps a landmark when paired with the *Casey* case because of Kennedy's vote of fidelity to that decision. But it was definitely not a turn to the left. Instead, it was a nonturn further to the right, a signal that this Court was satisfied with the balance it struck a generation ago. The undue-burden test of *Casey* allowed states to enact all but the most extreme restrictions on women's access to abortion. Texas had taken full advantage. From that year until 2011, the rate of abortion in the state dropped by 43 percent (in the same period, the rate throughout the United States dropped by 34 percent).

According to the Guttmacher Institute, a woman in Texas who wants to have an abortion needs to have abortion counseling designed to discourage her from doing that and then wait twenty-four hours before she can have the procedure. She has to undergo an ultrasound before obtaining an abortion, and the provider has to show and describe the image of the fetus to the woman. If she is a minor, she needs consent from a parent and has to notify her parent before having an abortion. She can get public funding for an abortion only if her life is endangered, she has been raped, or she has engaged in incest.

If Breyer and the others in the Court majority had wanted to push back against the tide of conservative antiabortion legislation in Texas and elsewhere, rather than judging only the consequences of the two unconstitutional provisions, they would have focused on the first element of the undue-burden test in the *Casey* opinion—when "a state regulation has the purpose" of burdening "a woman seeking an abortion." They would have called the bluff of the Texas legislature and said plainly that the wording and detail about women's health and safety were a pretext—and an illegitimate one—for making it much harder for them to get abortions and that an illegitimate purpose was as unconstitutional as an illegitimate effect.

If Breyer had been writing only for himself, that would have been a striking omission. As a justice, he had crusaded for the Supreme Court, and courts in general, to figure out through the history of legislation as well as its text the intentions or purpose of legislatures when they pass laws. "That's the democratic way," Breyer said. But in the Texas case, Breyer was also writing for Kennedy and the other justices in the majority. Kennedy's investment in *Casey* likely included its limits on abortion, as well as its respect for *Roe*'s "essential holding."

For the Court as a political as well as a legal institution, the decision was nonetheless very significant. In Texas, the abortion regulations the Court struck down were the result of fierce conservative political efforts—a fresh antiabortion surge carrying on the long campaign against a woman's right to choose since *Roe v. Wade* came out of the state forty-six years earlier.

If the Court had upheld the two regulations, it would have affirmed Texas's pretexts and provided additional evidence that it was political in the most extreme sense, a rubber stamp for extreme policy flouting the law of

the land. Instead, it tempered politics into law of consequence by establishing a precedent for reconsidering laws
in twenty-four states that go beyond what is necessary to
ensure the safety of patients. It was a dramatic victory for
women and for American medicine.

The Texas affirmative action case, *Fisher v. University of
Texas at Austin*, contained another surprising Kennedy
vote, his first supporting an affirmative action program in
twenty-eight years on the Court. From the shorthanded
Court of eight, Elena Kagan was recused from taking part
in the case, presumably because she had worked on it as
solicitor general, the post she held for sixteen months
before joining the Court in 2010. It was almost certain that
the outcome of the case would be 4–3, with the three consistent conservatives on one side, the three liberals on the
other, and Kennedy the fourth vote.

What remained uncertain was whether Kennedy
was open to the possibility that the university's program was
constitutional, since it allowed the admissions office to
take race into account in evaluating a candidate's application. Lyle Denniston, the dean of the Supreme Court
press corps, wrote on SCOTUSblog that the result in the
case could "make it unconstitutional for public universities and colleges to take race into account in any way in
choosing their entering classes."

The case was returning to the Court for the second
time in three years. In 2013, for a majority of 7–1, Kennedy
wrote the opinion sending the case back to the Fifth Circuit for a more searching scrutiny of the program. Kennedy had proposed that level of scrutiny in a dissent in

2003 in the Court's previous major case about affirmative action. He wrote then, "The Constitution cannot confer the right to classify on the basis of race even in this special context absent searching judicial review." Affirmative action has been among the most divisive of the wedge issues in American politics and in constitutional law for almost as long as abortion. Major institutions in this society, like Fortune 500 corporations, the US military, and leading colleges and universities, have said how essential it is for helping them maintain the diversity they prize. Powerful political efforts have skillfully pushed back, outlawing affirmative action at public universities in eight states.

Rather than guiding the country through this thicket of politics and law, the Supreme Court had stumbled through it, creating confusion for lower courts and reflecting the country's contradictory feelings about this difficult and yet, from the perspective of major institutions, often useful policy. The saga of the *Fisher* case showed how politics seemed to overtake law at the Court. There was no conflict in the circuit courts for the Supreme Court to resolve when the petition arrived there for the first iteration of the case. It was a political case targeted at the conservatives on the Court for them to end a chapter in the law by doing what Denniston said they might.

As the appeals court interpreted the decision in the 2013 *Fisher* case, the Supreme Court had not changed the core principles of its support for affirmative action in higher education—"that a university can have a compelling interest in attaining the educational benefits of diversity, and that its admissions program must be narrowly tailored to serve this interest." But it had "altered the application of those principles in a critical way. Now, courts must give 'no deference'" to a university program, the appeals court said: "Put simply, there is no special form of strict scrutiny unique to higher education admissions decisions."

On that basis, the Fifth Circuit again upheld the Texas program by 2–1. So did the Supreme Court, with Kennedy writing the opinion for the Court. Like his vote in the abortion case, his vote in the affirmative action case was widely interpreted as a significant sign of his shift to the left. Again, as political scientists would code the case, it was a liberal victory. Because he was in the majority in eighty-one of the eighty-three cases that the Court decided during the 2015 term—98 percent of the time—his vote determining the outcome in the case was interpreted as a sign of the Court's shift to the left, as well.

But the opinion was not a ringing endorsement of affirmative action. Instead, it was a narrow affirmation of the Fifth Circuit's decision and of a program that Kennedy called *"sui generis"*—and therefore no model or basis for a broadly applicable precedent—because it was used to fill only 25 percent of the university's freshman class. It was another clear example of how the Republican Court's rightward shift in the previous almost half a century had moved the meaning of a liberal outcome to the right.

In relating the history of affirmative action at the university from 1996 to the present, Kennedy laid out how embattled the program had been virtually the whole time. Twenty years before, the Fifth Circuit had struck down an affirmative action program at the University of Texas Law School, rejecting the fundamental basis for using race as a factor in admissions in the Supreme Court's landmark 1978 *Bakke* ruling—diversity.

The Fifth Circuit said then that "classification of persons on the basis of race for the purpose of diversity frustrates, rather than facilitates, the goals of equal protection." The Supreme Court chose not to review that ruling, so for seven years—until 2003, when the Court reconfirmed that affirmative action was constitutional throughout the United States—Texas, Louisiana, and Mississippi, the states comprising the Fifth Circuit, operated under a different law from the rest of the country.

Beginning in 1998, the university began to use a Top Ten Percent plan passed by the legislature, guaranteeing a place at any of the public universities in Texas to anyone in the top 10 percent of his or her high school class. That was seen as a sensible political compromise, though not an ideal educational one. As Justice Ruth Bader Ginsburg pointed out, plans like this one "encourage parents to keep their children in low-performing segregated schools, and discourage students from taking challenging classes that might lower their grade point averages."

In 2004, after a university study concluded that this supposedly race-neutral approach was not providing enough educational benefits of diversity, the university adopted its current plan, admitting 75 percent of the incoming class through the Top Ten Percent plan and the rest through the so-called holistic plan, in which Texas uses race as a factor in admissions, along with socioeconomic status and other special circumstances of applicants. Texas based its plan on the approach the Court endorsed in 2003, "a highly individualized, holistic review of each applicant's file, giving serious consideration to all the ways an applicant might contribute to a diverse educational environment."

Kennedy is known as the Court's most persistent proponent for dignity as a value protected by the Constitution. In this instance, however, he invoked that value as a reason for caution about affirmative action rather than enthusiasm. He wrote, "[I]t remains an enduring challenge to our nation's education system to reconcile the pursuit of diversity with the constitutional promise of equal treatment and dignity."

Rather than endorse the Texas program, his opinion put the university on notice about its obligation to continue scrutinizing its diversity efforts: "The Court's affirmance of the University's admissions policy today does not necessarily mean the University may rely on that same policy without refinement. It is the University's ongoing obligation to engage in constant deliberation and continued reflection regarding its admissions policies."

The 2015 affirmative action ruling was similar to the abortion ruling in underscoring that the Court is a legal as well as a political institution. Kennedy's vote in support of an affirmative action program for the first time in his very long career as a justice was a vote for respecting the essential holding that affirmative action can meet the stringent standards for it that the Court has set. It was a vote against the campaign of his conservative colleagues to end affirmative action at colleges and universities—colleagues who had voted to rehear the University of Texas case when, under the Court's conventions, there was no reason to. But it also emphasized how grudging the Court's case law is about affirmative action when, measured by any benchmark of achievement, meaningful equality remains a distant dream for many blacks and other minority groups in America.

In the abortion and affirmative action cases, Solicitor General Don Verrilli submitted influential briefs and made helpful oral arguments on behalf of the winning parties, though the US government was not a party in either case. Why he did provides an insight about the relationship between politics and law at the Supreme Court and how elite opinion about that changed in the last generation. In 1987, I published a book called *The Tenth Justice: The Solicitor General and the Rule of Law*. It is about the group that Verrilli recently led from the 2011 term through the 2015 term, the Office of the Solicitor General in the US Justice Department, which represents the president and the federal government before the Supreme Court. The book told how—as part of the Reagan administration's effort in the 1980s to bring about major changes in social policy through the federal courts by persuading them to outlaw abortion, end affirmative action, and accomplish similar goals—the Reagan team at the Justice Department politicized the office.

The first solicitor general (SG) in the administration was Rex Lee, a traditional conservative from Utah who believed that he should not ask the Court to overturn a controversial precedent if he thought a majority of the Court was unlikely to do that. After he was hounded out of office, he defended himself by saying that his job had been to be the solicitor general, not the "pamphleteer general."

Lee's belief in gradualism before the Court continued a tradition of SGs of both major political parties. Archibald Cox, who was SG for the Democratic Kennedy administration, shared Lee's attitude. Lawyers with cases before the Court where the government was not involved often asked the SG to file a friend-of-the-Court (amicus) brief on behalf of their client, because the SG's imprimatur was so influential. Cox was reluctant to do that unless there was a tangible federal interest in the case. He defined that narrowly, so he filed such briefs in only 20 percent of the cases he took part in. The other 80 percent were cases where the government was a party.

Charles Fried, who succeeded Lee as the Reagan administration's SG, took a more spacious approach to defining the federal interest. In his first term as SG, the office filed amicus briefs at a rate of almost 50 percent of the government's filings for most of the term, until the rate dropped off to 41 percent later that Court year.

One way to understand the difference between the Cox and Fried approaches is that Cox hewed to a conception of law as separate from politics and held the line at 20 percent to maintain what he saw as that separation as fully as possible. Fried, on the other hand, perceived that in many cases, there was only a blurry line between law and politics or no line at all. The more cases the SG's office took part in, the more influential it could be. The amicus brief was a tool of change.

Between 1965, which was Cox's last year as SG, and the end of the 2015 term, the docket of the Supreme Court eventually fell from about 140 cases to about 80—with a spike inbetween to around 175 cases. But the participation of the SG's office has grown notably from about 55 percent of the Court's docket in the Cox years to about 82 percent of the docket now: lawyers from the SG's office are the ultimate repeat players at the Court.

And that office now files more briefs as a friend of the Court than as a party: 57 percent versus 43 percent.

In a law-review article about this phenomenon, Margaret Meriwether Cordray and Richard Cordray found that solicitors general of both parties have taken part as a friend of the Court only in "cases that directly and substantially affect the federal government's institutional interests." But they observed: "Given the extensive reach of the federal government's involvement in modern life, it is perhaps not surprising that the Solicitor General can articulate a substantial interest in most of the Court's cases." That is a reach that Fried perceived in the 1980s and that Cox did not twenty years before.

In representing the president and the federal government, the solicitor general has the job where politics and law regularly come together before the Court. There has never been a question about who the SG works for: the president picks the SG as a political appointee. But the SG is informally called the Supreme Court's tenth justice because, as Justice Lewis Powell put it, the lawyer in the post is considered to have a "dual responsibility" that includes helping the Court find the right path for the law.

In Cox's time, followers of the SG's office saw no tension between those responsibilities: the president and his attorney general deferred to the SG to carry them out as he saw fit. In Fried's time, the tension was apparent. Some followers of the SG's office were concerned that the Reagan administration was undercutting the office's credibility in other cases, with aggressive advocacy in cases about its social agenda.

Now, once again, there is little or no tension—but for a different reason. Each administration, Democratic or

Republican, has its agenda cases, which are distinct from other cases the SG's office handles. The Court expects Republican administrations to argue for abortion restrictions and Democratic administrations to argue against them. In addition, there are cases where, though the government is not a party, it has a strong policy interest, and the number of those cases is now regularly bigger than the number of cases where the government is a party. During the past generation, the law has made room for politics and so has the Office of the Solicitor General. In its formal way, it has adjusted to the generally accepted presumption that the work of the Supreme Court involves politics as well as law.

The last case that the Court heard argued, in April, was *McDonnell v. United States*. It was also one of the last the Court decided and was the most perplexing. Unanimously by 8–0, with the chief justice writing for the Court, it overturned the conviction of former Virginia governor Robert F. McDonnell on eleven counts of corruption. His wife, Maureen McDonnell, was convicted of eight counts of corruption and one count of obstruction of an official proceeding, but she appealed separately, and her appeal was not before the Court.

This was a clear victory for white-collar criminal defendants—a liberal outcome. But the case was perplexing because the closer you looked, the more contradictory it seemed. The facts seemed to make it clear that McDonnell knew what he was doing and that what he was doing involved a *quid pro quo*.

The legal ruling highlighted the Court's role as a political institution in the uncontroversial sense of making decisions that shape the workings of the political branches of government. But the facts and the unanimity of the decision left room for the impression that the Court was acting politically in an unsavory and controversial sense—by protecting the access of insiders to government, the flexibility of politicians to help them, and a level of ingratiation, as scholars call it, from insiders to politicians that only very wealthy insiders can provide.

Between 2009 and 2012, while he was governor and a rising star in the national Republican Party, McDonnell and his family received $175,000 in gifts, loans, vacations, and other benefits from Jonnie Williams, a Virginia businessman. Williams—the chief executive officer of Star Scientific, a company in the state—was pushing to get approved as a pharmaceutical a nutritional supplement called Anatabloc, which the company had developed from a chemical compound in tobacco, and to get Virginia's public universities to perform research studies that would help secure that approval.

The opinion for a unanimous panel of three judges on the Fourth Circuit upholding McDonnell's convictions spent eighteen pages reciting the facts of the case. When McDonnell was elected governor in 2009, he was fifty-five, and his financial situation was shaky. Through a company that he and his sister owned called Mobo Properties, they were losing $40,000 a year on two beachfront rentals in Virginia Beach. (By 2012, they owed $2.5 million in loans on them.) When he was inaugurated in January of 2010, McDonnell and his wife owed $74,000 on their credit cards. By September, the debt grew to $90,000.

McDonnell first met Jonnie Williams in New York City in December of 2009. The governor-elect wanted to thank Williams for use of his private plane during the gubernatorial campaign that fall. In October of 2010, while they flew together in the plane on a six-hour flight to California, Williams explained Anatabloc, which he and his company hoped would be proven to be an effective treatment for chronic inflammation. As he testified during McDonnell's trial, he told the governor "that what I needed from him was that I needed testing and I wanted to have this done in Virginia." By the end of the flight, they agreed that "independent testing in Virginia was a good idea." The governor said that he would introduce Williams to Dr. William A. Hazel Jr., the state's Secretary of Health and Human Resources.

In April of 2011, McDonnell's wife invited Williams to join the couple at a political rally in New York City. When the governor-elect and Williams had met in December of 2009, Williams boasted that he knew Oscar de la Renta, the fashion designer, and had offered to buy from him a custom-made dress for McDonnell's wife to wear at the inauguration. McDonnell's chief counsel had nixed that: he called and said, "I understand that you're getting ready to purchase [Mrs.] McDonnell a dress for the inauguration. I'm calling to let you know that you can't do that." In 2011, when she called Williams, he recalled while testifying, she said, "I'll have you seated with the governor and we can go shopping now."

Williams took her shopping in New York. He bought her a dress at Bergdorf Goodman. He bought her dresses and a white leather coat from Oscar de la Renta. He bought her shoes, a purse, and a raincoat from Louis

Vuitton. Altogether, he spent about $20,000 on her gifts. At the political rally that night, he sat with the governor and first lady of Virginia.

A few weeks later, they had a private dinner together at the governor's mansion to talk about William's product and the need for independent studies and testing. Two days after the dinner, Williams sent McDonnell's wife an e-mail with a link to an article titled "Star Scientific Has Home Run Potential," which discussed Star's research and stock. She forwarded this to the governor. Less than an hour later, he texted his sister, asking for information about the loans on their Mobo properties. He also e-mailed his daughter, asking her to send him information about bills he still needed to pay for her wedding.

The next day, Mrs. McDonnell and Williams met at the governor's mansion to discuss Anatabloc. But she began by explaining her family's financial woes. According to Williams, Mrs. McDonnell said, "I have a background in nutritional supplements and I can be helpful to you with this project, with your company. The governor says it's okay for me to help you and—but I need you to help me. I need you to help me with this financial situation."

Mrs. McDonnell asked to borrow $50,000. Williams agreed to loan the money to the McDonnells. She also said that she and her husband owed $15,000 for their daughter's wedding reception. Again, Williams said he would provide the money, but he called the governor to "make sure [he] knew about it." The governor's response was, "Thank you." Three days later, the governor met with his Secretary of Health and Human Resources and his chief of staff Martin Kent on state business. Shortly after the meeting, the governor forwarded to the secretary the article about Star that Mrs. McDonnell had sent him.

The opinion continued with similar details. Williams paid $2,380.24 for an outing for the governor, his two sons, and his soon-to-be son-in-law at Kinloch Golf Club in Virginia, where for more than seven hours, they played golf, ate, and shopped. McDonnell's wife went to Florida to attend a Star-sponsored event where she spoke to the audience, expressed her support for Star and its research, and invited the audience to the launch for Anatabloc, which would be held at the governor's mansion. Williams attended (and, in his plane, flew himself and the governor's children to) a retreat for McDonnell's political action committee, Opportunity Virginia, as "a $100,000 in-kind contributor to the campaign and the PAC," playing golf with the governor there and, after the retreat, sending golf bags with new clubs, plus golf shoes, to the governor and one of his sons.

The Fourth Circuit opinion recounted the governor directing Secretary Hazel "to have his deputy attend a meeting about Anatabloc with Mrs. McDonnell at the Governor's Mansion" and, at the meeting, Williams discussing clinical trials at the University of Virginia and Virginia Commonwealth University, the home of the Medical College of Virginia; Williams and Mrs. McDonnell meeting with Dr. John Clore from Virginia Commonwealth University; and "Williams—with Mrs. McDonnell at his side"—telling Clore "that clinical testing of Anatabloc in Virginia was important" to the governor.

The opinion continued, "After the meeting ended, Mrs. McDonnell noticed the Rolex watch adorning Williams's wrist. She mentioned that she wanted to get a

Rolex for Appellant"—the governor. "When Williams asked if she wanted him to purchase one for Appellant, she responded affirmatively." About two weeks later, "Williams purchased a Rolex from Malibu Jewelers in Malibu, California. The Rolex cost between $6,000 and $7,000 and featured a custom engraving: 'Robert F. McDonnell, 71st Governor of Virginia.' Mrs. McDonnell later took several pictures of Appellant showing off his new Rolex—pictures that were later sent to Williams via text message."

A couple of weeks later, the governor hosted a lunch paid for by his political action committee where Anatabloc was the focus. He asked researchers and others from Virginia's medical and scientific communities about the potential of the product and clinical testing of it. Williams began to hand out $25,000 for "grant applications" to doctors from different medical institutions. (The total was $200,000.)

In January of 2012, Mrs. McDonnell asked Williams for an additional loan because of the financial burden of the Virginia Beach properties. He agreed and, in the same conversation, mentioned that the University of Virginia studies of Anatabloc were moving slowly. She reported later to Williams that she had told the governor about the problem and that he wanted contact information for the people that Williams's company was dealing with at the university.

Williams did more along these lines for McDonnell and his wife. As governor and first lady, they did more to help Williams and Star and advance the validation of Anatabloc. The governor was convicted of engaging in fraud on the public by denying it the "honest services" of a public official because he had taken a bribe, of taking bribes in return for "official acts," and of conspiring to commit those crimes.

The gist of the Roberts opinion reversing the Fourth Circuit's decision and McDonnell's convictions and calling for a new trial was that while McDonnell and his family had enjoyed lavish gifts and more from Williams, the government had not proved that the governor used his authority to influence an outcome favorable to Williams. Roberts wrote, "There is no doubt that this case is distasteful; it may be worse than that. But our concern is not with tawdry tales of Ferraris, Rolexes, and ball gowns. It is instead with the broader legal implications of the Government's boundless interpretation of the federal bribery statute. A more limited interpretation of the term 'official act' leaves ample room for prosecuting corruption, while comporting with the text of the statute and the precedent of this Court."

The case turned on the meaning of "official act." Roberts defined it as "a formal exercise of governmental power that is similar in nature to a lawsuit before a court, a determination before an agency, or a hearing before a committee. It must also be something specific and focused that is 'pending' or 'may by law be brought' before a public official." That would include putting pressure on another official to carry out an "official act" or advising that official with the knowledge that the advice would form the basis of an "official act." But in all instances, an "official act" was a decision about, or a step of action affecting, a "question, matter, cause, suit, proceeding or controversy." Roberts concluded, "Setting up a meeting, talking to another official, or organizing an event (or agreeing to do so)—without more—does not fit" the definition of "official act."

The chief justice expressed some concern about the government's expansive conception of value received:

"[N]early anything a public official accepts—from a campaign contribution to lunch—counts as a *quid*." But he was very concerned about its expansive conception of value given: "[A]nd nearly anything a public official does—from arranging a meeting to inviting a guest to an event—counts as a *quo*."

He explained, "The basic compact underlying representative government *assumes* that public officials will hear from their constituents and act appropriately on their concerns—whether it is the union official worried about a plant closing or the homeowners who wonder why it took five days to restore power to their neighborhood after a storm. The Government's position could cast a pall of potential prosecution over these relationships if the union had given a campaign contribution in the past or the homeowners invited the official to join them on their annual outing to the ballgame."

Roberts was especially impressed by a friend-of-the-Court brief filed by, among other former government officials from both major political parties, "White House counsel who worked in every administration from that of President Reagan to President Obama." The brief argued that "an 'official action' for purposes of federal public corruption laws must be tied to an exercise of actual governmental power." It said that federal public corruption law "should not be broadened to subject government officials to the threat of prosecution for engaging in innocent conduct that occurs on a routine basis."

As Daniel Richman, a professor of law at Columbia University, and Jennifer Rodgers, the executive director of Columbia's Center for the Advancement of Public Integrity, wrote, "Any savvy observer would read this scenario as a pretty straightforward wooing of a Governor by a business owner and the sustained effort by a grateful but not heavy-handed Governor to put his Administration at the owner's disposal. And the connection between what McDonnell asked for and what he delivered could not have escaped the Governor, who, minutes after discussing with Williams a $50,000 loan McDonnell and his wife wanted, checked with the Governor's counsel about Anatabloc issues at Virginia's universities." He was the governor: he did not have to say, "I'm calling to pressure you."

But Richman and Rodgers also wrote,

> Obviously the newly narrowed definition of official action would apply to a retrial of the McDonnells themselves (if there is to be one). It is quite possible that a properly instructed jury would find that the Governor's actions did in fact constitute pressure on or advice to other officials on a qualifying question or matter. Or, a new jury might find that the Governor successfully threaded the needle; that by being courteous and encouraging but not bullying or overbearing he provided access to Williams that did not amount to commission of an "official act." Under the Court's analysis, the fact that McDonnell exercised the power of his office over state health and academic personnel at the request of, and for the benefit of, a financial benefactor would not support a conviction in the absence of a connection to something more than meetings.

At its core, the case was about faulty instructions to the jury in the McDonnell case, which "did not adequately explain to the jury how to identify the 'question, matter, cause, suit, proceeding or controversy'" that McDonnell's "official acts" were said to be affecting through the exercise of actual government power. The ruling was received as a major one, and it was: by a unanimous vote, the Court tightened the standard of proof that the government needs to meet to win a conviction for corruption.

The Roberts opinion tried to have that be the takeaway from the decision: "None of this, of course, is to suggest that the facts of this case typify normal political interaction between public officials and their constituents. Far from it. But the Government's legal interpretation is not confined to cases involving extravagant gifts or large sums of money, and we cannot construe a criminal statute on the assumption that the Government will 'use it responsibly.'"

Yet the opinion bolstered the view that the Court was protecting insiders and politicians by listing the current and former political officials who favored it: "Six former Virginia attorneys general—four Democrats and two Republicans—also filed an *amicus* brief in this Court echoing those concerns, as did 77 former state attorneys general from States other than Virginia—41 Democrats, 35 Republicans, and 1 independent."

In this case, the Fourth Circuit's decision that the Supreme Court overturned was far more convincing: "The temporal relationship between the 'quids' and 'quos'— the gifts, payments, loans, and favors and the official acts— constitute compelling evidence of corrupt intent."

The most significant Roberts opinion of the term came in *Foster v. Chatman*, not in the *McDonnell* case. By 7–1, with the chief justice writing for the majority, the Court overturned a decision of the Georgia Supreme Court and found that Timothy Tyrone Foster met the standard he needed to, to appeal his conviction for capital murder and his sentence of death.

It was a death penalty case, but more dramatically, it was a case about race and an example of how even when the Court comes together in strong agreement and makes a legal ruling with moral force, it cannot escape having its decision connected to the most visceral form of politics unfolding on America's streets.

The petition to the US Supreme Court that persuaded it to hear his case said, "Foster was a poor, black, intellectually compromised eighteen-year-old when he was charged in 1986 with murdering Queen White, an elderly white woman who worked as a school teacher before her retirement." At his trial in 1987, there were forty-two prospective jurors, only four of them black. The prosecution used four of the ten strikes it was allowed to remove all the blacks, so the jury that heard Foster's case and that convicted and sentenced him to death was all white.

The year before the trial, by 7–2, in *Batson v. Kentucky*, the Court had ruled that racial discrimination in selecting jurors in criminal cases deprives the defendant of important rights during a trial and is devastating to the community because it "undermines public confidence in the fairness of our system of justice." When a defendant makes a good case that the prosecution has removed a potential juror because of his race, the Court ruled, the prosecution must have a "neutral" reason for excluding the person, or the strike violates the Constitution.

Among defense lawyers, *Batson* is widely considered a failure, because courts are rarely willing to find that prosecutors intentionally discriminated and then lied about that by making up a neutral, or nonracial, reason. Pretexts are rampant in this area of the law. But Foster had a strong case because his lawyers were able to obtain notes from the prosecution, which showed obvious racial discrimination. The case as it reached the Court focused on two of the black prospective jurors.

On the list of prospective jurors, the names of the blacks were highlighted in green, and a legend said the green "represents Blacks." The letter B was also next to each of those prospective jurors' names. There were handwritten notes about three of the black prospective jurors, identified as "B#1," "B#2," and "B#3," and on a handwritten document titled "definite NO's" with six names, the first five were of the four black prospective jurors in the case, plus a fifth who dropped out of the pool. Other notes provided similar evidence that the prosecution had identified the black prospective jurors and had planned to strike them because of their race.

The two the *Foster* case focused on were Marilyn Garrett and Eddie Hood. Roberts wrote that in justifying his decision to strike Garrett, the prosecutor provided "a laundry list of reasons": she "(1) worked with disadvantaged youth in her job as a teacher's aide; (2) kept looking at the ground during *voir dire*; (3) gave short and curt answers during *voir dire*; (4) appeared nervous; (5) was too young; (6) misrepresented her familiarity with the location of the crime; (7) failed to disclose that her cousin had been arrested on a drug charge; (8) was divorced; (9) had two children and two jobs; (10) was asked few questions by the defense; and (11) did not ask to be excused from jury service."

The trial court accepted the prosecutor's reasons, Roberts went on, but his examination of the record revealed "that much of the reasoning" provided by the prosecutor had "no grounding in fact." The prosecutor told the court that he had considered Garrett as a juror and had made up his mind to strike her only at the last minute. That "was false," Roberts wrote, because the prosecution "from the outset was intent on ensuring that none" of the black prospective jurors on its list would be allowed to serve on the jury. "In short," Roberts went on, "contrary to the prosecution's submissions, the State's resolve to strike Garrett was never in doubt."

Roberts's analysis was similarly granular about the prosecution's strike of Hood. "With respect to both Garrett and Hood," he summarized, "such evidence is compelling. But that is not all. There are also the shifting explanations, the misrepresentations of the record, and the persistent focus on race in the prosecution's file. Considering all of the circumstantial evidence that 'bear[s] upon the issue of racial animosity,'" he went on, quoting a landmark Court precedent in this area of law, "we are left with the firm conviction that the strikes of Garrett and Hood were 'motivated in substantial part by discriminatory intent.'"

He concluded, "Two peremptory strikes on the basis of race are two more than the Constitution allows."

The Roberts opinion condemned intentional racial discrimination in the selection of a jury without doing much to prevent it in other cases. But as Stephen B. Bright, the president of the Southern Human Rights Center and the lawyer who won the case in the Supreme Court, told me, "*Foster* may encourage some appellate courts" to scrutinize more carefully the reasons that prosecutors give to justify seemingly discriminatory strikes. It emphasized the value of side-by-side comparisons of black jurors struck and white jurors accepted. It also found the strikes of Hood and Garrett invalid even though the prosecutors gave many reasons for each strike, which meant that lower courts could no longer hold, as many have done, that if one reason was "race neutral," there was no *Batson* violation even if any other reason showed bias.

But the ruling did not fix the problems of *Batson*. It showed concern about discrimination while allowing it to continue in all but few cases. Discrimination would likely remain rampant in jury selection. The narrowness of the *Foster* holding compared to the breadth of racial discrimination in jury selection and apparent throughout the criminal justice system was a reminder of Roberts's insistence in a series of Court opinions that it should not allow systemic remedies for racial discrimination.

In 2007, in the first major ruling of the Roberts Court, the chief justice wrote, "The way to stop discrimination on the basis of race is to stop discriminating on the basis of race." In that case, the Court struck down student assignment plans in Louisville, Kentucky, and Seattle, Washington, which sought to maintain racial diversity in individual schools through measures that took explicit though limited account of a student's race.

The Court was deeply divided, with Justice Breyer in dissent calling the decision a "radical" rejection of well-settled law allowing for modest, voluntary actions, especially by democratically elected school boards. The chief justice of the United States was insisting that the government can and should wish away historical and continuing inequities by asserting that it is time our society started acting as if it is color-blind: that reflected a willful blindness to a tenacious and supremely important challenge in American life, as tragedy after outrage manifestly about race have made very clear.

The Court decided other politically charged cases in October Term 2015.

Montgomery v. Louisiana. By 6–3, it extended a 2012 holding saying that its ban on life without parole as punishment for juveniles applied to a thousand or more inmates whose sentences had become final by the date of that decision. The Court also expanded that holding by raising the chances that a defendant has an opportunity to show he or she does not deserve life without parole. The Court said that that punishment is unconstitutional for a juvenile, unless he or she is found to be "irreparably corrupt" or "permanently incorrigible." It was an example of how the generally conservative Court has retreated from the heavy emphasis on retribution and has moved to the left on some criminal justice issues like much of the rest of the country.

Evenwel v. Abbott. Unanimously by 8–0, the Court ruled that the Constitution does not require states to set up voting districts by the number of eligible voters in each one. The Court answered the question of whether the half-century-old standard of "one person, one vote" required that or allowed the state of Texas to have voting districts roughly equal in population, as every state does. The Court did not answer whether Texas or another state would be allowed to use a measure other than total population, and it did not require what the solicitor general asked it to, by saying that the Constitution requires states to set up districts based on total population. About a politically charged subject, the Court made a narrow legal ruling, which reflected a split among the justices evident at the oral argument between deferring to the states to decide the question for themselves and enunciating a constitutional standard.

Utah v. Strieff. By 5–3, the Court further undermined the exclusionary rule, maintaining the longtime rule of conduct that evidence obtained in an illegal search is inadmissible in court as "fruit of the poisonous tree," while all but creating a new exception to the rule for searches made without a warrant on someone who turns out to have a warrant outstanding against him already. Writing for the majority, Clarence Thomas stated that the "exclusionary rule does not apply when the costs of exclusion outweigh its deterrent benefits." Once again, a rule of decision had gotten the better of a rule of conduct, and the politics of law and order had gotten the better of the law. In dissent, Elena Kagan noted the very large number of people who have outstanding warrants in the United States and said that the Court's ruling increased the incentive of police officers to stop individuals without reasonable suspicion— "exactly the temptation the exclusionary rule is supposed to remove."

Zubik v. Burwell. In an unsigned opinion, the Court announced its decision not to decide a case once considered among the term's most important. It was a challenge, based on religious freedom, to regulations that the Department of Health and Human Services devised under the Affordable Care Act about the mandate in the statute that employers provide their female employees with health insurance that offers free contraception. The regulations required that any religious nonprofit organization that objects to providing this coverage tell the government, so it can order the nonprofit's insurance company to provide the coverage at no cost to the employer.

In 2014, in the 5–4 ruling in *Burwell v. Hobby Lobby Stores*, the Court held that the Affordable Care Act violated a federal law protecting religious freedom by requiring a family-owned corporation to pay for insurance coverage of contraception. Samuel Alito, writing for the majority, said the ruling was limited to family-owned for-profit companies operated on religious principles. But the *Zubik* case—really, a group of cases brought by religiously affiliated social service organizations, hospitals, and universities—underscored that the ruling opened the door to a wide range of lawsuits. The case showed how politics sometimes uses law to bring about a major social change yet also to hide the effort.

The groups wanted the government to exempt them from the contraception mandate, like churches and other houses of worship. Instead, the government offered them a religious accommodation in the form of the notification, which the groups rejected because, they said, it made them complicit by deputizing a third party to sin on their behalf. So they brought their lawsuits.

Before Antonin Scalia's death, the uncertainty about the case was whether the Court would accept the accommodation that the government offered as a careful balancing of its respect for religious organizations and its responsibility to provide access to a full range of health benefits for everyone. After the oral argument in March, it seemed likely that the Court would split 4–4. That would have meant the nonprofits won in one US Circuit and lost in eight others.

The Court then did something extraordinary: it proposed a resolution to the case. A nonprofit, like the Little Sisters of the Poor Home for the Aged or Southern Nazarene University, would tell its insurance company that it did not want its plan to include coverage of contraception, and the insurer would offer (at no cost to itself) the nonprofit's employees that coverage. The government and the challengers said that was feasible, and the Court sent the cases back to the appeals courts to give the parties "an opportunity to arrive at an approach going forward that accommodates petitioners' religious exercise while at the same time ensuring that women covered by petitioners' health plans 'receive full and equal health coverage, including contraceptive coverage.'"

It was not a 4–4 tie, as happened in the immigration case and three and a half others, but it had a similar impact. The Court postponed a reckoning with the issue at the heart of the case until its ninth seat was filled. This political matter also postponed a public discussion about what that issue was. It appeared to be about the tension between religious freedom and health care. Since religious freedom is more contested today than it has been for a generation, it is no surprise that that value is being contested in the field of health care, too. But as the *Atlantic*'s Garrett Epps explained, it was really about how "'religious freedom' has morphed from a shield defending the meek into yet one more sword demanding obeisance to the haughty" by transferring power "from the less powerful party to the more powerful one."

In the *Hobby Lobby* case, the Court's conservative majority used the concept of religious freedom to protect a large commercial corporation from the requirement that health insurance policies for its employees cover contraception. Epps wrote, "[T]hat is a political belief, not a religious belief. It says, with a straight face, that government regulation offends my religion."

Politics had so effectively infiltrated the law that it was seen as something else. But in clouding the law, politics had reinforced the law's political side and the extent to which the permanent campaign in American politics had also become a recurring campaign at the Supreme Court.

The second most political case of the term, after the immigration case, was obscured by the flurry of rulings in June. Argued in January, decided in March, and called *Friedrichs v. California Teachers Association*, it was a 4–4 ruling that would almost certainly have been 5–4 with a conservative majority if Justice Scalia had not died. Instead, the equally divided result left in place the Ninth Circuit ruling that the conservatives would have overturned.

On the surface, the case was a challenge by a group of California teachers who had resigned as members of the state's teachers union and did not want to pay a fee to support its collective bargaining with the state as the exclusive representative of all teachers, union members or not. The Christian Educators International, a nonprofit religious organization, joined the teachers as plaintiffs. Beneath the surface, however, it was as politically charged as *Citizens United*.

The substance of the appeals court ruling said in full, "Upon review, the court finds that the questions presented in this appeal are so insubstantial as not to require further argument, because they are governed by controlling Supreme Court and Ninth Circuit precedent." The appeals court upheld a similar ruling of the federal district court in the case, because the precedents were so clearly against the position the challengers asked the lower courts to take.

From a 1977 Supreme Court decision called *Abood v. Detroit Board of Education*, the law was that the shop of a union chosen to negotiate exclusively on behalf of the city's public teachers could require a teacher to pay a service fee, even if the person was not going to join the union, to cover the costs of collective bargaining, contract administration, and so forth. (It is called an agency fee or a fair-share fee or plan.) Otherwise, that teacher and others would benefit from those services as free riders, without paying for them, and that would jeopardize "labor peace."

The plaintiffs knew their position was a loser: theirs was a test case, brought by the libertarian Center for Individual Rights. As the trial judge wrote in the order doing what the center asked, "Before the Court is Plaintiffs' Motion for Judgment on the Pleadings, requesting that judgment be entered in favor of Defendants." They entreated the lower courts to rule against them quickly so they could take their case to the Supreme Court and petition it to overrule *Abood*.

Justice Alito had all but invited this challenge in a 2012 case called *Knox v. Service Employees International Union, Local 1000*. The Court ruled then that a public-employees union had infringed on the free-speech rights of nonmembers by not giving them the chance to prevent their dues from being used to support expressions of political views unrelated to collective bargaining. In his majority opinion, Alito wrote that "we do not revisit today whether the Court's former cases have given adequate recognition to the critical First Amendment rights at stake"—but he came close to saying that the Court would like to hear from parties with the same kind of issue so it could revisit the question.

In the *Knox* case, in a parallel to their aggressiveness in *Citizens United*, the five justices in the conservative majority did what no party had asked for and no lower court had considered, breaking the Court's own rules. They required that the union replace its opt-out clause— which allowed a nonmember to opt out of paying a 25 percent increase in fees to fight antiunion policies—with an opt-in clause. The only way a nonmember would be asked to pay a share of the increase was by choosing to—by opting in. Without that shift, there was "a risk that the fees nonmembers pay will be used to further political and ideological ends with which they do not agree." The Court held that "the compulsory fees constitute a form of compelled speech and association that imposes a 'significant impingement on First Amendment rights.'"

In 2014, in the related case of *Harris v. Quinn*, with Alito again writing for the Court, the conservative majority ruled that a state law could not require personal assistants providing care at home to Medicaid patients to pay a fee to a public-employees union as their representatives in collective bargaining. The First Amendment, he said, does not permit a state "to compel personal care providers to subsidize speech on matters of public concern by a union that they do not wish to join or support." The Alito opinion said the case was not governed by the *Abood* decision, since personal assistants were only quasi-public employees: the state paid them, but they worked for the people they cared for. The opinion attacked *Abood*, however, in another obvious invitation from the conservative majority for challengers to ask the Court to overturn the precedent. In his *Knox* and *Harris* opinions, Alito fused two previously distinct elements of union activity to create a weapon for use against public unions. Since shortly after World War II, the Court has permitted states to make contracts with unions, designating them as exclusive representatives of a group of public workers and allowing them to require nonmembers to pay a fee covering collective bargaining and similar job-related activities. But unions cannot charge nonmembers for political activities, like supporting a candidate for public office.

Alito essentially said there is no difference between job-related and political activities for unions representing public employees. As government workers, their pay and benefits are matters of politics. Requiring nonmembers to pay a union fee to cover collective bargaining is the same as requiring them to pay for support of a political candidate. He was taking up the right-to-work crusade against unions, which, as of July 2016 (when West Virginia became the twenty-sixth state to institute a right-to-work law) has now triumphed in more than half the states.

Justice Kagan answered Alito's *Harris* opinion with a dissent worth quoting at length. This passage is a fair sample of her prose as the most effective writer on the Court:

> *Abood* is not, as the majority at one point describes it, "something of an anomaly," allowing uncommon interference with individuals' expressive activities. Rather,

the lines it draws and the balance it strikes reflect the way courts generally evaluate claims that a condition of public employment violates the First Amendment. Our decisions have long afforded government entities broad latitude to manage their workforces, even when that affects speech they could not regulate in other contexts. *Abood* is of a piece with all those decisions: While protecting an employee's most significant expression, that decision also enables the government to advance its interests in operating effectively—by bargaining, if it so chooses, with a single employee representative and preventing free riding on that union's efforts.

For that reason, one aspect of today's opinion is cause for satisfaction, though hardly applause. As this case came to us, the principal question it presented was whether to overrule *Abood*: The petitioners devoted the lion's share of their briefing and argument to urging us to overturn that nearly 40-year-old precedent (and the respondents and amici countered in the same vein). Today's majority cannot resist taking potshots at *Abood*, but it ignores the petitioners' invitation to depart from principles of *stare decisis*. And the essential work in the majority's opinion comes from its extended (though mistaken) distinction of *Abood*, not from its gratuitous dicta critiquing *Abood*'s foundations. That is to the good—or at least better than it might be. The *Abood* rule is deeply entrenched, and is the foundation for not tens or hundreds, but thousands of contracts between unions and governments across the Nation. Our precedent about precedent, fairly understood and applied, makes it impossible for this Court to reverse that decision.

She went on:

For many decades, Americans have debated the pros and cons of right-to-work laws and fair-share requirements. All across the country and continuing to the present day, citizens have engaged in passionate argument about the issue and have made disparate policy choices. The petitioners in this case asked this Court to end that discussion for the entire public sector, by overruling *Abood* and thus imposing a right-to-work regime for all government employees. The good news out of this case is clear: The majority declined that radical request.

When the Court decided to review the *Friedrichs* case, the impetus from the *Knox* and *Harris* decisions led to wide expectation among Court-watchers that the conservative majority would rule that the First Amendment prohibits government from forcing public employees to support unions in any manner, including when they engage in collective bargaining. The Court explicitly asked the parties to address whether *Abood* should be overruled.

During the oral argument in January, however, Justice Ginsburg raised a different topic with David C. Frederick, the lawyer for the union. She asked, "Mr. Frederick, you didn't ask for this judgment. It was thrust on you, this judgment on the pleadings. You did say you wanted to make a record in the district court. If you had had that opportunity to develop a record, what would you have put in it?"

He replied, "Well, the first thing I would have put in, it would have been a response to Justice Kennedy's question, which is that Ms. Friedrichs"—Rebecca Friedrichs, the lead plaintiff—"has said publicly she's happy with the positions the union is taking on pay. It would be anomalous to suppose that we're going to decide a case of this kind of constitutional import with a lead plaintiff who has said publicly she agrees with the union's positions on pay."

The justice suggested how the case was like *Citizens United*: as a vehicle for overturning established precedent. Apparently, the conservative justices seized on a case that lacked a factual record against which to test the validity of that law. And as with *Citizens United*, the justices in the conservative majority seemed poised to use the First Amendment for a partisan purpose, eager as they were to use it as a weapon against unions of public employees.

If their view prevailed, it would be a serious blow to public unions, which represent around 35 percent of the country's twenty million public employees, or more than seven million people. Their view aligned with that of the Republican Party and of conservative foundations that have long supported the antiunion, right-to-work campaign, as Kagan's view supported by the other liberal justices aligned with that of the Democrats.

Scalia's death left the conservatives and liberals deadlocked. That defused the case. But the impasse was a reminder that *Citizens United* was no anomaly and that the political Court was only temporarily in enforced repose while it waited to plot its new course with a ninth justice.

Chapter 5

The Death Penalty

Antonin Scalia's final opinion for the Supreme Court, in *Kansas v. Carr*, was about the death penalty. Scalia wrote for the majority in an 8–1 ruling that overturned a decision of the Kansas Supreme Court. During his last decade on the bench, Scalia had grown impatient with all the ways that the Supreme Court had delayed executions. The Kansas case dealt with an issue that had especially galled Scalia—for a quarter of a century, since his early years on the Court. The issue was mitigation and the Court's holding that a jury weighing whether to impose a death sentence must consider any extenuating circumstances about a defendant that would make a death sentence unjust.

In *Courting Death: The Supreme Court and Capital Punishment*, the sister-and-brother team of Carol S. Steiker of Harvard Law School and Jordan M. Steiker of the University of Texas Law School wrote that the "death penalty has political character as a symbol" because it is "a focal point of fears of violent crime" and "a shorthand for 'law and order.'" It has political character as a product—as a penalty in a state law, as the punishment for an offense that a prosecutor charges in a trial, or as the sentence that a jury imposes—because "some or all of the most important actors in the administration of capital punishment are elected." That includes state legislators who pass death penalty laws, state governors and attorneys general who carry them out, state prosecutors who bring capital charges, and state judges who preside over death penalty cases or review them on appeal.

Much of the Court's disagreement about the death penalty has reflected the deeply political nature of the issue. The disagreement has largely come in the era of the Republican Court because, until shortly before this period, the Court left it to each state to decide whether it wanted to have the death penalty as a punishment for crime. On the Republican Court for almost thirty years, Scalia was the most vehement defender of capital punishment. During that time, evidence mounted that states with the death penalty were struggling and failing to carry it out according to legal standards devised by the Court. Yet Scalia regularly fought the view that if states could not carry out capital punishment constitutionally, it must be unconstitutional. The fight he waged about the seemingly narrow issue of mitigation illustrates how, because of his conviction that capital punishment is constitutional, he felt justified in refusing to accept that a part of the law governing the death penalty was settled even when a majority of the Court said it was.

Since 1976, the Court has required that a defendant charged with a crime for which he could be sentenced to death be given a two-part trial: the first, to determine whether he is guilty of the crime; the second, if he is convicted, to decide whether to impose a death sentence. In the second, a jury is required to consider the defendant's circumstances and not to define him by his crime. The jury can sentence him to death only if it finds that in addition to committing the crime, there was some aggravating factor making it worse—for example, that the victim he murdered was a police officer.

The jury can choose to sentence him to life in prison, rather than to death, if there is a mitigating factor—say, that he had an intellectual disability that restricted his capacity to understand the consequences of his attacking the officer. The 1976 opinion for the Court included this key sentence, with a long buildup to a memorable climax: "A process that accords no significance to relevant facets of the character and record of the individual offender or the circumstances of the particular offense excludes from consideration in fixing the ultimate punishment of death the possibility of compassionate or mitigating factors stemming from the diverse frailties of humankind."

A major issue that Scalia's Kansas opinion addressed was whether it was constitutional for Kansas jurors to sentence a person to death, even though the judge failed to tell them explicitly that they could choose the alternative of sentencing the defendant to life in prison—and that they could do that even if the defendant's lawyer did not prove the mitigating evidence beyond a reasonable doubt. The instruction to the jury was a rewording of a portion of the Kansas statute about sentencing. The instruction went like this: "The state has the burden to prove beyond a reasonable doubt that there are one or more aggravating circumstances and that they are not outweighed by any mitigating circumstances found to exist."

This was a highly technical issue with life-or-death consequences. In finding the instruction acceptable under the Constitution, Scalia struck a confident—even breezy—tone: "The juxtaposition of aggravating and mitigating circumstances, so goes the argument, caused the jury to speculate that mitigating circumstances must also be proved beyond a reasonable doubt. It seems to us quite the opposite. The instruction makes clear that both the existence of aggravating circumstances and the conclusion that they outweigh mitigating circumstances must be proved beyond a reasonable doubt; mitigating circumstances themselves, on the other hand, must merely be 'found to exist.'"

In dissent, Justice Sonia Sotomayor proposed a very different way of thinking about the instruction. In 2001 and again in 2008, the Kansas Supreme Court ordered that jury instructions in the state's trial courts say what Kansas state law requires, which is that a lawyer for the defendant had to prove mitigating circumstances only to the satisfaction of an individual juror—not beyond a reasonable doubt. The state's instructions were finally changed to say that in 2011, so the case that the Supreme Court decided involved outmoded instructions: they were from the period before state prosecutors complied with the Kansas Supreme Court's directive. To Sotomayor, the part of the US Supreme Court's ruling that dealt with this issue was superfluous, because it had been resolved and was likely to have no bearing on other states.

Scalia also upbraided the Kansas Supreme Court for invalidating death sentences imposed by Kansas trial courts and for doing that "time and again." The State Supreme Court deserved a scolding twice over, Scalia implied: repeatedly, he suggested, it had chosen to review and strike down death sentences that should have been allowed to stand; and in those cases, it had written that the US Constitution required it to overturn those sentences when, according to the US Supreme Court, its decisions said otherwise. The "time and again" was misleading on both levels: the Supreme Court had reviewed and overturned only two other cases in which the Kansas Supreme Court invalidated a death sentence imposed by a Kansas trial court; and the Kansas court had invalidated few death sentences, because the state's trial courts seldom imposed the death penalty.

After the US Supreme Court struck down death penalty laws throughout the country in 1972 and reinstated capital punishment by approving revised laws in 1976, Kansas did not pass a new death penalty law until 1994. Since then, capital charges had been filed in eighty-five cases by the time Scalia's Kansas opinion became public. Twenty-six of the cases went to trial. Juries sentenced thirteen of the defendants to capital punishment. While their cases were on appeal, three made plea deals for life without parole. A fourth died in prison. The nine others were behind bars while appealing their sentences.

The last four executions in Kansas happened more than a half century ago, in 1965. Kansas is on the list of states that maintain the death penalty, yet at the time of Scalia's opinion, the state was literally not prepared to use it. The state's Department of Corrections had no plans to execute any offender. It had no protocol for execution when an offender exhausted his appeals. By law, the Kansas Supreme Court is required to review every death sentence imposed in state court. Its opinions in death penalty cases had shown that Court to be centrist and workmanlike— not, as Scalia implied, gung-ho to protect the liberty of the men sentenced to death by reading unintended meaning into US Supreme Court decisions.

Scalia's irritation with the Kansas Supreme Court reflected his deep disapproval of the US Supreme Court's doctrine about mitigating factors in death penalty cases.

In 1990, at the end of his fourth year on the Court, by 5–4, the Court upheld the death penalty statute of Arizona, with Scalia in the majority. But it upheld one part of the statute by a plurality of only four justices. (A plurality is the largest group of justices voting together in a decision.) They upheld the requirement that a defendant had to establish, by a preponderance of the evidence, the existence of a mitigating factor substantial enough to justify leniency from a court and a sentence of life in prison.

Scalia kept that four from being a majority of five because he chose that moment to reject the Court's doctrine about mitigating factors. When the Court reinstated the death penalty in 1976, he summarized, it established the principle that the discretion of a trial court in applying the death penalty "must be suitably directed and limited so as to minimize the risk of wholly arbitrary and capricious action." But in a related case that day, it also established another principle that "a defendant could not be sentenced to death unless the sentencer was convinced, by an unconstrained and unguided evaluation of offender and offense, that death was the appropriate punishment."

The premise of the second principle was that someone who commits a crime resulting in part from an intellectual disability may not deserve the death penalty because he is less culpable than someone who lacks that excuse. But Scalia offered the opinion that this principle has severely limited states' "discretion to decide that an offender eligible for the death penalty" should receive it.

It was common among death penalty experts to recognize that there was a tension between requiring limited discretion in applying the death penalty, to avoid having it be used capriciously yet requiring unlimited discretion in considering mitigating evidence, to avoid having the penalty imposed on someone who did not deserve it. Scalia was derisive about that view. He wrote that it was "rather like saying that there was perhaps an inherent tension between the Allies and the Axis Powers in World War II." He concluded, "They cannot be reconciled." The purpose of his concurrence was to show "that our jurisprudence and logic have long since parted ways" and to explain why he would "no longer seek to apply" the second of what he considered "the two incompatible branches of that jurisprudence." Dramatically, in 1990, he rejected a line of precedents going back to 1976.

Of the more than 2,800 cases he took part in on the Court, at least seventy-five dealt with the death penalty, depending on whether cases about related issues are included. Among the seventy-five, he voted with the majority in about two-thirds of the cases yet wrote the majority opinion in only a handful. His views rarely reflected the opinion of the majority. Tenaciously, he favored capital punishment. As tenaciously, he generally opposed constraints on it, which he expressed in many concurring opinions and dissents.

He was certain that the Constitution allows the death penalty because that fundamental law refers to it explicitly—in the Fifth Amendment ("No person shall be held to answer for a capital, or otherwise infamous crime, unless on a presentment or indictment of a Grand jury.") and in the Fourteenth (No person shall "be deprived of life, liberty, or property, without due process of law."). His ideal for the death penalty was that each state should wield it, or not, as the state chooses.

More important, he was disdainful of the Court's efforts to regulate how states administer the death penalty system so it is applied fairly and consistently—by attempting to discipline it. He urged severe restrictions on the ability of people to challenge their death sentences. He was dismissive of concerns that other justices expressed about innocent people being wrongly sentenced and put to death—even though, between 1976 and the end of 2015, 156 people convicted of murder and sentenced to death were later exonerated.

Scalia's rejection of the line of precedents about mitigating factors was at the other end of the spectrum from the rejection that Justices William J. Brennan Jr. and Thurgood Marshall made of capital punishment. After the Court reinstated it in 1976, in every subsequent death penalty case until each stepped down (Brennan in 1990, Marshall the following year), they each wrote some version of, "Adhering to my view that the death penalty is in all circumstances cruel and unusual punishment prohibited by the Eighth and Fourteenth Amendments, I would vacate the death sentence in this case."

Scalia was not on the Court when they began their long train of dissents, so he could not respond to them. But when Justice Harry A. Blackmun, in his twenty-fourth and final year on the Court in 1994, made a similar declaration, Scalia retorted. The well-known sentence of Blackmun's opinion is: "From this day forward, I no longer shall tinker with the machinery of death." The passage it introduces goes on like this: "For more than 20 years I have endeavored—indeed, I have struggled—along with a majority of this Court, to develop procedural and substantive rules that would lend more than the mere appearance of fairness to the death penalty endeavor. Rather than continue to coddle the Court's delusion that the desired level of fairness has been achieved and the need for regulation eviscerated, I feel morally and intellectually obligated simply to concede that the death penalty experiment has failed."

Scalia's retort was scalding: "Convictions in opposition to the death penalty are often passionate and deeply held. That would be no excuse for reading them into a Constitution that does not contain them, even if they represented the convictions of a majority of Americans. Much less is there any excuse for using that course to thrust a minority's views upon the people."

The view of the Court's majority, as Scalia interpreted it, was that the death penalty remained on the books because "the people" believed that "more brutal deaths may be deterred by capital punishment" and that the Constitution's cruel-and-unusual clause in the Eighth Amendment allowed that. The people also believed that the clause allowed maintaining the punishment, if they "merely conclude that justice requires such brutal deaths to be avenged by capital punishment."

He illustrated his polemic with examples of deaths to be avenged by execution. One was "the case of the 11-year old girl raped by four men and then killed by stuffing her panties down her throat. See *McCollum* v. *North Carolina*, No. 93-7200, cert. now pending before the Court. How enviable a quiet death by lethal injection compared with that!"

But twenty years later, the McCollum of that case, Henry Lee, was exonerated, along with his half brother, Leon Brown. In 1983, the eleven-year-old girl had been raped and murdered as Scalia described, in the town of

Red Springs, North Carolina. Otherwise, the implications he made about McCollum and Brown were inaccurate. At the time of the crime, McCollum was nineteen years old and mentally challenged. His IQ was later tested as low as fifty-one. Brown was fifteen years old and similarly challenged. His IQ tested as low as forty-nine. The first time the police questioned McCollum, he said he had seen the girl walking to a store around noon the day before she was raped and murdered. The next time, they fed him information about the crime and browbeat him into signing a confession. Brown signed one soon after. They were charged with rape and capital murder and put in prison. A year later, they were convicted based largely on their confessions. There was no physical or forensic evidence linking either to the crime.

After years of effort by lawyers on their behalf, technicians did DNA testing on a cigarette butt found near the girl's body. The DNA profile didn't match McCollum's or Brown's. It did match that of another man named Roscoe Artis, who was serving life in prison for a string of sexual assaults. He had told another inmate that McCollum and Brown were innocent. The other inmate told their lawyers that Artis "knew some obscure facts about the crime, including the color of the victim's underwear and how she was killed." In 2014, after years of legal efforts, North Carolina's Center for Death Penalty Litigation requested that the convictions of McCollum and Brown be vacated. The charges against them were dismissed. They were released at the ages of fifty and forty-six, after thirty-one years in prison—the 144th and 145th convicted of capital crimes, sentenced to death, and later exonerated, by the end of 2015. North Carolina's governor pardoned them.

Scalia's polemic against Blackmun's dissent was tripped up by facts, as the death penalty has been repeatedly since 1976.

In 1966, according to the Gallup Poll, for the only time in the past eighty years, more Americans opposed the death penalty than supported it: 47 percent versus 42 percent. Over the next several years, supporters outnumbered opponents, but the division was relatively even. Violent crime in the country was low, and the number of death sentences and executions had fallen precipitously in the generation since the 1930s. That set the stage for the modern era of the death penalty in the United States.

In 1972, when the Court struck down the death penalty as it existed then in the country by 5–4, it did not rule that capital punishment was unconstitutional. But a common view was that the ruling marked the end of capital punishment in the United States. Still, the clash between the majority and the dissenters reflected the abiding dispute in the country about the punishment.

Even the five justices in the majority disagreed with each other about the basis for the ruling: Brennan and Marshall wrote that it was time to rule capital punishment unconstitutional, as "degrading to human dignity" (Brennan) and shocking to the average citizen's "conscience and sense of justice" (Marshall). Justices William O. Douglas, Potter Stewart, and Byron White generally agreed that the death penalty was being applied in arbitrary, capricious, and discriminatory ways. No justice joined the opinion of any other among the five.

The decision provoked a defiant backlash. As support for the death penalty climbed and opposition fell, thirty-five states passed new laws imposing capital punishment in the next four years. A few of the laws said the death penalty was mandatory for anyone convicted of committing a so-called capital crime, like murder, rape, or kidnapping. The Supreme Court struck those down.

Most of the new state laws adopted a version of the Model Penal Code developed by the American Law Institute, the nonpartisan law-reform group composed of judges, scholars, and lawyers. In states that had the death penalty, the code's goals were to provide guidance to prosecutors about whether to seek a death sentence and to jurors about whether to impose it. In providing that, the aim was to solve the main problem of the state laws struck down four years earlier: by lacking guidance about who the laws should be applied to, they left those choices to the subjective judgments of prosecutors and jurors.

In 1976, the Court upheld the ALI approach to the death sentence and treated the high number of new state death penalty laws as evidence that capital punishment reflected current standards of decency in the United States. The majority endorsed careful application of capital punishment, so only the worst of the worst would receive a death sentence. In effect, the Court was constitutionalizing the punishment—regulating it under the Constitution.

As the Steikers explain in *Courting Death: The Supreme Court and Capital Punishment*, this was something new in American law and unprecedented in any country, a distinct alternative to abolition and retention. It began a lengthy experiment. Decades of evidence lead to the conclusion that the experiment has failed badly. Many states have imposed the death penalty in ways that discriminate by race and geography. Countless juries have been confused about how to weigh critical evidence in capital cases, like whether they should regard proof of a defendant's intellectual disability as a reason not to impose a death sentence or to execute him. Thousands of trial courts have made serious legal mistakes on their way to imposing a death sentence and have been reversed by appeals courts. Thousands of lawyers unprepared for the demanding nature of the work have given slipshod counsel to people charged with capital crimes.

One state after another has botched an execution by lethal injection, leading to apparently excruciating pain for the men being executed and a growing sense that states cannot properly carry out the only form of execution that a majority of Americans have said is acceptable. The death penalty has become enormously costly. An authoritative study in California underscored the high expense of prosecuting capital cases, defending people charged with capital crimes, and housing people on death row: between 1978 and 2011, when the state executed only thirteen people, the cost of administering the death penalty there was $4.04 billion.

According to the Justice Department, of the 8,124 people sentenced to death between 1977 and 2013, 17 percent were executed, 6 percent died by causes other than execution, and 40 percent received other dispositions, including reversals of their convictions. The rest—37 percent—were in prison. In California in 2014, a federal judge found that of the 748 inmates then on the state's death row, more than two out of every five had been there for twenty years or longer.

Courting Death argues that, having set rules about the administration of the death penalty under the Constitution that many states have not been able, or willing, to comply with, the Supreme Court should decide that capital punishment is unconstitutional. Justice Stephen Breyer cited the Steiker's scholarship at the end of the 2014 term in a significant dissent. He wrote, "[R]ather than try to patch up the death penalty's legal wounds one at a time," the Court should recognize "that the death penalty violates the Eighth Amendment"—the constitutional clause prohibiting the infliction of "cruel and unusual punishments."

The most striking testimony the Steikers presented in support of this position came from five Supreme Court justices, appointed by Republicans as well as Democrats, who at one time voted in favor of the death penalty and, based on what they learned as justices about the miscarriages of the death penalty system, changed their minds.

They have done that while still on the bench or after they retired. They include former justices Lewis F. Powell Jr., Harry A. Blackmun, and John Paul Stevens, plus current justices Breyer and Ruth Bader Ginsburg. Adding in William J. Brennan Jr. and Thurgood Marshall—who are well known for having opposed the death penalty on moral grounds— the Steikers write that seven justices have "explicitly stated that they think capital punishment should be ruled categorically unconstitutional."

Scalia's experience took him in the opposite direction. In 1989, by 5-4, the Court rejected the argument that the death penalty should not be imposed on sixteen- or seventeen-year-olds. Scalia was in his third year as a justice and wrote the plurality opinion for himself and three other justices. He emphasized that the Court had to look to "the conceptions of modern American society as reflected by objective evidence," not to the Court's "own subjective concepts," to determine the country's evolving standards of decency. He found that there was no "settled consensus against the execution of 16- and 17-year-old offenders."

Sixteen years later, in 2005, again by 5–4, the Court overturned that decision. Justice Anthony Kennedy wrote the majority opinion. The majority found that thirty states prohibited the so-called juvenile death penalty—eighteen that maintained the death penalty but excluded "juveniles from its reach" and twelve that had no death penalty. The majority also found that in the twenty states "without a formal prohibition," the execution of juveniles was "infrequent." That squared with the view that "juvenile offenders cannot with reliability be classified among the worst offenders," because their "susceptibility to immature and irresponsible behavior means their irresponsible conduct is not as morally reprehensible as that of an adult." Kennedy wrote that to the extent the 1989 decision had been based on "review of the objective indicia of consensus" at the time, "it suffices to note that those indicia have changed."

Scalia dissented, aiming to fillet Kennedy's reasoning, lay out how the Court should have addressed and resolved the issue, and attract attention by accusing the majority of exercising power it did not have. He accepted that the Court had "long rejected a purely originalist approach to our Eighth Amendment" and its prohibition against cruel and unusual punishment—his view that future generations had to figure out what people would have regarded as cruel and unusual when the Constitution was ratified in the late-eighteenth century. But on its own terms, Scalia argued—"the Court having pronounced that the Eighth Amendment is an ever-changing reflection of the evolving standards of decency of our society"—that its job was to "discern them from the practices of our people" and not to "*prescribe* those standards" (he used italics for emphasis).

"On the evolving-standards hypothesis," he wrote, "the only legitimate function of this Court is to identify a moral consensus of the American people. By what conceivable warrant can nine lawyers presume to be the authoritative conscience of the Nation?" He summarized, "What a mockery today's opinion makes" of the idea that the Court was bound down by rules and precedents. He went on, "Today's opinion provides a perfect example of why judges are ill equipped to make the type of legislative judgments the Court insists on making here."

The core of Scalia's contention was that "the subjective views of five Members of this Court" should not determine the Eighth Amendment's meaning—that the Court's view should be based on "objective indicia," which he defined as "practices of our people." The fundamental difference between the majority and Scalia was about how to interpret those practices. He was especially critical of the majority for including in its tabulation of the thirty states that prohibited the death penalty for people under eighteen the dozen states that prohibited the death penalty for everyone: "That 12 states favor no executions says something about consensus against the death penalty, but nothing—absolutely nothing—about consensus that offenders under 18 deserve special immunity from such a penalty."

About one of the most divisive issues in American politics during the era of the Republican Court, it had decided that the most persuasive grounds for its legal rulings about capital punishment were political decisions by the states. But when evidence from politics convinced a majority of justices to change the law by narrowing whom the death penalty applied to, Scalia disagreed about the meaning of that evidence.

The 8–1 vote of the US Supreme to overturn the Kansas Supreme Court was a puzzling outcome, because the Sotomayor dissent was correct that the ruling dealt with an outmoded jury instruction making the issue superfluous: it had been resolved and was likely to have no bearing on other states. It seemed likely that one or more of the liberal justices who joined Scalia's majority opinion did so for strategic reasons: they did not want to call attention to the division on the Court about the death penalty by joining Sotomayor's dissent when, on the fundamental question whether the Court should find capital punishment unconstitutional, the case was irrelevant.

But in Kansas, it was not. The state is one of the many in the United States that relies on retention elections to hold their justices accountable: a merit-selection system chooses them and, after a justice's first year in office, he or she is subject to a retention vote in the next general election; if a majority of voters elect to retain the justice, he or she remains in office for a term of six years and stands in another retention election at the end of each term. Since this system went into effect in 1958, no justice had been voted out of office in a retention election through 2015. No justice had proved inept, unethical, or otherwise unfit for service on the Kansas Supreme Court. But in 2014, two justices were retained by thin margins. They were targeted for joining the majority of the Court in the death penalty case that the US Supreme Court later overturned in the 2015 term. "Judges in states with retention elections," the scholars Brandice Canes-Wrone, Tom S. Clark, and Jee-Kwang Park recently found, "showed no sign of being insulated from public opinion."

In 2016, five of the Court's seven justices are up for retention, four of them targeted for similar attack. There has been a political campaign in Kansas against the State Supreme Court in recent years because, in a series of decisions, it has held that the state has inadequately funded its public schools. The Republican governor and the Republican-dominated legislature have been livid about these rulings. They have been eager to take over the Court by removing a majority of the justices and replacing them with partisan allies. But it is hard to stir voters with attack ads about school funding. The death penalty is a much more provocative goad.

The 2014 retention elections in Kansas proved that. In the 2016 elections, Kansans concerned about the threat to the independence of the Kansas Supreme Court expect that Scalia's scolding of the Court in his final opinion will be used against those four state justices. The politics of the US Supreme Court are likely to play a serious role in the politics about the Kansas Supreme Court. But Scalia's death raises the prospect of the Supreme Court reckoning soon with the death penalty's legal wounds and deciding whether it is time for it to end its failed effort to regulate the penalty under the Constitution.

Citizens and the Court

Before the start of the 2015 term, according to the Pew Research Center, the percentage of Americans surveyed with a favorable opinion of the Supreme Court (48 percent) was lower than it had been in thirty years, and the percentage with an unfavorable rating (43 percent) was higher. Republicans were largely responsible for the unfavorable rating. A high percentage of them (61 percent) viewed the Court unfavorably—up a lot from only a few months before (40 percent). While only a modest percentage of Republicans (33 percent) had a favorable view, a high percentage of Democrats did (62 percent).

The results of the Pew survey reflected views of the Court as a political institution—one that makes policy decisions—and other public opinion polls corroborated them. A Gallup Poll around the same time found that 50 percent of people surveyed disapproved of how the Supreme Court was handling its job, compared to 45 percent who approved.

The major rulings of the previous term were about the Affordable Care Act—the signature legislation of the Obama administration—and about same-sex marriage. By 6-3, with Roberts writing for the majority, the Court found that people who are self-employed or unemployed and buy health insurance through an exchange set up under the act can get subsidies, whether a state set up the exchange or the federal government set one up because a state declined to. By 5–4, with Kennedy writing for the majority, the Court ruled that the fundamental right to marry under the Constitution applies equally to people of the same sex throughout the United States.

The views of Republicans and Democrats generally reflected the views of their political parties about the outcomes in those and other politically defined cases. A high percentage of conservative Republicans (68 percent) saw the Court as liberal, so the percentage of Americans who held that view was at its highest number in almost a decade (36 percent). A low percentage of conservative Republicans (5 percent) saw the Court as conservative.

The percentage of all Americans, conservatives and liberals, who held the view that the Court was conservative was at its lowest number in almost a decade (18 percent), down by half in that period. More liberal Democrats viewed the Court as middle-of-the-road (49 percent) than conservative (30 percent) or liberal (17 percent). A Pew report commented: "[O]pinions about the court and its ideology have never been more politically divided."

That did not mean they were well informed. A common view among polling experts is that when Americans are surveyed about the workings of government, including the Court, they do not know much. They have opinions framed by current news, and they shape those opinions drawing on their prior experiences—as justices do. In responding to the Court's major rulings as if they were pieces of legislation reflecting outcomes in policy, most of the people that Pew surveyed said they regarded the justices as doing the same. A high percentage (70 percent) said that the justices were "often influenced by their own political views." Only a small percentage (24 percent) said that justices "generally put their political views aside" when deciding cases. Yet most of the people were apparently not bothered by the wide perception that the justices' political views often influenced their decisions. By a small majority (54 percent), the people surveyed said that the Court had the right amount of power, though a sizable minority (36 percent) said it had too much power. Republicans (45 percent) were more likely than independents (33 percent) or Democrats (32 percent) to regard the court as too powerful.

Surveys like Pew's are one kind of information that scholars and journalists rely on in assessing the Supreme Court. They are called performance evaluations and measure "specific support." The other kind of information that scholars and journalists use is about institutional support, or "diffuse support." It has provided the main counter to the performance evaluations. Especially compared with other parts of government, the argument goes, the Supreme Court has generally enjoyed a reservoir of goodwill among Americans. That has moderated jumps in disapproval after unpopular or controversial rulings, the counter continues, so extreme shifts in public opinion about the Court, like those that Pew recorded and reported before the start of the 2015 term, are often misleadingly negative.

The scholars James L. Gibson, Gregory A. Caldeira, and Vanessa A. Baird have written, "Simply put, to know courts is to love them, because to know them is to be exposed to a series of legitimizing messages focused on the symbols of justice, judicial objectivity, and impartiality." In other words, when justices frame their work as "a process of deducing outcomes from first principles"— Scalia: "To hold a governmental act to be unconstitutional is not to announce that we forbid it, but that the *Constitution* forbids it"—people tend to believe that.

Gibson, at Washington University, is a proponent of "positivity theory," which focuses on "the legitimizing role of the symbols of judicial authority." In a 2016 paper, he and Michael J. Nelson of Pennsylvania State University argued that despite reports from organizations like Pew about how much the reputation of the Supreme Court has plummeted, there is "an important moderating role of the symbols of judicial authority through which the Court's legitimacy is protected. When people are simultaneously exposed to an unwanted decision and legitimacy-reinforcing symbols, the effects of disappointment with the unwanted decision are *eliminated*." To get this result, the researchers used such symbols as a photo of the temple-like Supreme Court building, a photo of the Court's nine justices before Scalia died, and a photograph of a judge's gavel.

But the Gibson-Nelson report contained these caveats:

> Most Americans get most of their political news from television. We suspect that most television reports on Supreme Court decisions are accompanied by images of the Justices, the Court, and the other symbolic paraphernalia of the legal system. Our evidence indicates that, absent these symbols, disappointment with a Court decision can harm the institution's legitimacy.

However, instances where people learn about disappointing rulings without exposure to judicial symbols may not be particularly common. The experimental condition most closely connected to reality—the one presenting judicial symbols—is one in which the effects of decisional disappointment are nullified. Symbols therefore seem to play a formidable role in sustaining judicial legitimacy.

Assume that most Americans get their political news from television—a 2016 Pew report found that 57 percent of Americans did—but that they do not get much news about the Supreme Court. That is a prudent assumption, according to a study by the scholars Marc J. Hetherington and Joseph L. Smith. Though it was published in 2007—so it is dated by almost a decade—its logic is convincing. They found that strong support for the Court among liberals continued long past the time it became a conservative institution. That would have made sense if the public had moved to the right along with the Court, but since the early 1980s, the Court has been notably more conservative than the American public.

According to Hetherington and Smith, liberals continued to like the Court more than conservatives because they did not know much about its decisions and were not motivated to learn about them. "To the extent that the public knows about specific decisions," they wrote, "they know much more about dated ones than recent ones." One reason is that the media in the period they studied paid a lot more attention to old rulings than recent ones. Between 1991 and 1997, they found, the *New York Times* mentioned the 1973 landmark *Roe v. Wade* 603 times and mentioned *Planned Parenthood v. Casey*, the 1992 ruling that restricted a woman's right to choose, only 59 times.

When the Court makes significant decisions, it is rarely out of sync with the majority of the American people—or so many political scientists have found. In *The Will of the People*, his history of the role of public opinion in shaping the Court, Barry Friedman wrote, "The accountability of the Justices (and thus the Constitution) to the popular will has been established time and time again." Hetherington and Smith have nonetheless concluded that except when it rules in major cases, "the public is unlikely to notice that the Court has strayed far from its preferences." Neither political science nor legal scholarship has convincingly figured out a reliable way to measure how the public regards the Court. Public opinion about it rises and falls with the popularity of outcomes in recent major cases, which means that judgments about it resting on public opinion are not really judgments about the Court.

Instead, they are judgments about policy, or politics. Institutional support—the diffuse kind that is said to counterbalance public opinion—is measured by approximations. It suffers from the same weakness as the Pew survey, by measuring only a piece of the Court's work. That is not a criticism of Pew or its research, which is a valuable public service. But students of the Supreme Court sometimes use that kind of data for a purpose it was not meant to serve.

Because 2016 is an election year, Pew's summer survey after the end of the 2015 term concentrated on politics, not politics and the Court. But it included a question about the Court and showed a large change from the year before in its overall favorable and unfavorable ratings—62 percent and 29 percent, respectively, up from 48 percent and down from 43 percent.

The major rulings of the term driving the volatility of the ratings were about abortion rights and affirmative action. The decision on abortion rights simply reinforced the twenty-four-year-old ruling that cut back on *Roe*'s protections and allowed many abortion restrictions; the decision on affirmative action simply restated the weak support for it by the Court and its reading of the Constitution. But the jump in the Court's popularity and the drop in its unpopularity showed that people had adjusted to those realities. They approved that the decisions were not departures from what they had adjusted to.

In the absence of a less volatile and more reliable measure of the Court's standing, surveys that rate the Court's decisions as policy—or political—outcomes reinforce its identity as a political institution. That is a good thing because it is generally accurate, but it is bad because it reflects only part of the truth. It is also bad because the meaning of politics in American life during the last decade has changed drastically.

Before Barack Obama was elected president, most Americans regarded their political inclination as one of many personal characteristics, like where they are from, and it was generally low on that list. Now people's identities as Republicans or Democrats often define them and drive their attitudes about social and other prominent matters, including about the outcomes in major Court cases. This may explain why Republicans have recently been so critical of the Court even though it has long been and, until Scalia's death, remained a largely Republican Court.

Because most people have no direct experience with the Supreme Court, G. Evans Witt, the chief executive officer of Princeton Survey Research Associates International, told me that what people know about it is from news and opinion polls and focuses on the Court's partisan divide. "The fight over the Garland nomination has been incredibly destructive to the public view of the Court," he said, "because it has reinforced the sense that the Court is a partisan institution." It did not matter that Garland was uniformly considered an excellent judge: the public saw him as a Democratic judge. In Witt's view, that attitude could only be fixed by the Court, by it deciding some politically fraught cases by 7–2, 8–1, or even 9–0 margins. Otherwise, he said, attitudes about the Court will remain the same.

On the other hand, Chief Justice Roberts and many in the legal establishment have carried out a "crusade to exterminate 'politics' from the judiciary," as Charles Geyh of Indiana University's Mauer School of Law described it. Every time someone insists that law and politics are separate—Roberts: "We don't work as Democrats or Republicans"—the public grows more convinced either that it's being deceived or that the speaker is self-deceived.

Uncertainty about how to measure the standing of the Court matters because every theory about its role in American life treats its standing—the Court's legitimacy—as its primary test. Legitimacy is far too important a concept to rest on such imprecise, debatable, and slim judgments.

What should be done to strengthen the Court's legitimacy and encourage acceptance of the reality that it is both a political and a legal institution?

First, the Senate's advise-and-consent process for making judgments about a Supreme Court nominee should be changed to include questions that provide a fuller understanding of his or her approach to interpreting the Constitution and other forms of law. For the past sixty years, since it has become a tradition for the Senate Judiciary Committee to question a nominee, it has been accepted that the nominee should not answer any question about a specific case because, as Sandra Day O'Connor told the Committee in 1981 during her confirmation hearing, that "would mean that I have prejudged the matter or have morally committed myself to a certain position."

Robert Post and Reva Siegel of Yale Law School have proposed a solution to this problem, "a method of questioning that will enable the Senate to evaluate the constitutional commitments of nominees while preserving the independent integrity of the law." They believe that Senators should "ask nominees to explain the grounds on which they would have voted in past decisions of the Supreme Court."

As they explained, "[T]he purpose of such questions is *not* to bind future interpretive judgments of nominees." Rather, the "Senate should expressly affirm that its questions are solely for the purpose of clarifying a nominee's constitutional philosophy, and that a nominee's answers would not be construed as any kind of promise or guarantee of how the nominee would vote in future cases." That "should not compromise the independence of the Court, but instead should contribute to the democratic legitimacy that is its necessary precondition."

In *The Next Justice*, Christopher L. Eisgruber, president of Princeton University, offered another way to probe a nominee's judicial philosophy—by asking about role models ("What twentieth-century justice's jurisprudence do you most admire and why?"), about judicial review ("What purposes do you think it serves? In other words, when and why is it a good thing to have judges intervening in the political process of a democratic country?"), and about how to interpret the Constitution ("When do you believe that Justices should enforce rights such as the right to travel, or the right to marry, or the right of parents to guide the upbringing of their children, which are not mentioned explicitly in the Constitution?") A nominee would be free to duck the questions, but "those evasions" would give senators "a legitimate ground for rejecting the nomination."

Second, the Constitution should be amended so that, instead of life terms, justices are appointed for eighteen-year terms, with appointments staggered every two years. Every president serving a full four-year term would appoint two justices, with the advice and consent of the Senate. Presidents would also appoint a justice to fill out the remaining time in the term of any justice unable to complete it.

In making this change, the country would recognize that as a political institution, the Court should reflect the constancy and change of national politics—and avoid an outcome like the current one where the presidents of one party have appointed twelve of the sixteen most recent justices. If this plan had been in effect in those years, there would have been twenty-four justices appointed—fourteen by Republican presidents, ten by Democrats.

The change should also reduce the strife in the confirmation process, by making appointment and confirmation an every-other-year practice. The chief justice could be the most senior justice or the median justice (with four justices more senior and four less senior) or chosen some other way to avoid the kind of one-party leadership of the last almost half century.

This routine would strengthen incentives for the political parties to make the selection of justices a high priority for every candidate for the presidency and for the Senate. Presidential candidates have sometimes campaigned against the Court, as Franklin D. Roosevelt did during the Depression and as Richard M. Nixon did in 1968. But presidential candidates have rarely campaigned for it by describing their view of the Court's role or of the ideal justice. Both are too important to leave to a president's undisclosed preferences. Candidates must feel obliged to say the kind of Court and justice they favor and why.

Third, the Supreme Court should adopt the Code of Conduct for United States Judges as the judicial code for justices. The controversy that Justice Ginsburg stirred up with her comments about Donald Trump in the summer of 2016 should never have happened—and it would not have happened if justices were bound by the code. In recent years, questions about justices' ability to judge impartially in cases have come up frequently enough that they are an earnest concern of experts on judicial ethics. The Court leaves to each justice the decision whether to recuse himself or herself from a case, which means that in each instance, a justice violates a basic principle of ethics by serving as the judge in his or her own case.

Stephen Gillers, a legal ethics expert who teaches at New York University Law School, proposed a sensible recusal process that would not limit the Court's independence. A recusal motion from a party in a case before the Court would go to the justice involved and the chief justice as the reviewer—or to the senior associate justice, if the motion was about the chief. If the justice decided not to recuse, the justice reviewing the decision would either agree or disagree and, if he or she concluded that the motion had merit, would refer it to the full Court for a final decision—without the justice who received the motion. Any decision by the Court would require a written opinion, and it would take a majority of the reviewing Court to call for recusal. Recusal motions are rare, so the Gillers proposal would not add much to the Court's workload.

In 2012, hundreds of law professors signed a letter asking the justices to adopt the code voluntarily and to change how they handle requests for recusal. A coalition of government watchdog groups supported the letter by gathering and delivering to the Court one hundred thousand signatures in favor of the letter's proposals. Taking this step would strengthen the Court's legitimacy. If the Court does not take it, Congress may do so under the same authority that would allow it to change the size of the Court through legislation.

Fourth, journalism's conception of Court coverage must expand to take fuller account of it as a political as well as a legal institution. Anthony J. Lewis established the dominant approach of current Court coverage when he reported on it from 1957 to 1964 as a correspondent for the *New York Times*. In the *Journal of Supreme Court History*, in 2004, the University of Texas's L. A. Powe Jr. wrote: "Lewis was the pioneer, the first reporter to see Supreme Court decisions, not just as a won-loss, but instead as part of a continuing constitutional process where reasons and reasoning mattered."

Sixty years later, reporters for leading outlets have built on this tradition for the general audience interested in public affairs and for the specialized legal audience. SCOTUSblog, the website devoted to coverage of the Court, embodies this approach by collecting all the filings and judicial opinions in every case decided by the justices, along with history, explanation, and analysis of the case. Lewis spent a year as a student at Harvard Law School as a Nieman Fellow to work out how he would go about his coverage. Many of the top reporters on the Court today have law degrees. Their mastery of substance and procedure is evident in their work.

What's often largely missing, however, is the context of cases: the path through politics of a policy turned into law; the controversy, if any, about that process and what got emphasized, distorted, or left out as a result; the larger social and economic currents that influenced the politics around the policy and law; and the full legal history shaping the case. The basic insight of the field of judicial politics is that the Court is one of the key institutions making policy in American governance, not the only one, and that it needs to be understood in relation to the other players.

"Change does not just begin at a point in time," Lewis emphasized. "It builds on history." Some people covering the Court incorporate that essential element in their reporting. But ironically, what is generally left out of journalism is what once defined the field of judicial politics within political science and has been eclipsed by empirical scholarship.

Two generations ago, Robert McCloskey was widely known for his classic work *The American Supreme Court*, which approached the Court as a political and legal institution. The book is now in its fifth edition, with new material by the University of Texas Law School's Sanford Levinson. The approach deserves to be widely emulated by journalists, so their work will provide a fuller account of the Court's role in American politics as well as law.

Fifth, David Cole's *Engines of Liberty* should be required reading for anyone thinking about the most important consequences of the Court being both a political and legal institution. He focused on the role in shaping constitutional law of what Justice Louis D. Brandeis called "the most important office": the private citizen. A century ago, during the Progressive Era, Brandeis was concerned about "serious injury to the public" if citizens were to neglect their civic duties. For his part, Cole focused on the upside—the power Americans have when they fully engage as citizens. His book showed that a combination of political and legal advocacy is a basic way for citizens to tell the Supreme Court what they think the Constitution should mean.

Cole demonstrated that recent Court rulings perceived as thunderbolts of newly found law—in 2015, the holding that the Constitution guarantees a right to same-sex marriage; in 2008, the ruling that it guarantees a right of individuals to own guns for personal use; and in the 2000s, rulings that the US government owes rights of due process to enemy combatants in a US war against terrorists—were actually products of organized and long-standing citizen campaigns. Cole built on a central idea in Larry Kramer's *The People Themselves* that for Supreme

Court justices, "there is a higher authority out there with power to overturn their decisions—an actual authority, too, not some abstract 'people' who spoke once, two hundred years ago, and then disappeared."

Early failures in these efforts, Cole argued convincingly, were critical in working out political arguments that could sway public opinion and then in developing corresponding legal arguments. By his reckoning, the gay marriage ruling was twenty years in the making, the gun rights ruling thirty, and the Gitmo rulings sixty. The last traces back to the Court's ignominious decision that the government could intern Japanese Americans during World War II, based solely on fear rather than proof of sabotage.

Cole's key point is that the will of the people is a product of politics, so it is essential to litigate in the court of public opinion before trying to win in court. Victories there, especially at the Supreme Court, depend on public opinion in most watershed cases. A giant exception is *Citizens United v. Federal Election Commission*. Cole argued that the way to overturn this plutocratic decision, now opposed by Republicans and Democrats alike, is through a grassroots campaign that catches on nationally, which is already under way in a few places and could help restore faith in the democratic process.

Sixth, the left needs to shape a coherent political-and-legal agenda to rival what the right shaped and sought to realize beginning in the Reagan era and continuing down to today. In their work in progress, *The Constitution of Opportunity*, Joseph Fishkin and William E. Forbath make the case for the importance of the idea of constitutionalism as a basis for politics, not the other way around. "As structures of opportunity grow more narrow and brittle, and class inequalities mount," they write, "our nation is becoming what reformers throughout the nineteenth and early twentieth century meant when they talked about a society with a 'moneyed aristocracy' or a 'ruling class'—an oligarchy, not a republic."

They go on: "The claim seems to raise constitutional concerns. And we think it should. For earlier generations of reformers, economic circumstances like our own posed not just an economic, social, or a political problem, but a *constitutional* one." To Fishkin and Forbath, the Constitution belongs at the beginning of the conversation about economics and inequality, about politics and policy—not the end: "Today, there remains broad agreement that it is important to promote opportunity, avoid oligarchy, and build a robust middle class. These principles remain mainstays of our politics. However, we have lost the crucial idea that these are *constitutional* principles."

Chief Judge Merrick Garland's opinion for the US Court of Appeals for the District of Columbia Circuit, in July of 2015, upheld a federal ban on federal contractors making federal campaign contributions. It begins with this prologue:

> Seventy-five years ago, Congress barred individuals and firms from making federal campaign contributions while they negotiate or perform federal contracts.
>
> The plaintiffs, who are individual government contractors, contend that this statute violates their First Amendment and equal protection rights. Because the concerns that spurred the original bar remain as

important today as when the statute was enacted, and because the statute is closely drawn to avoid unnecessary abridgment of associational freedoms, we reject the plaintiffs' challenge.

The case is about the most hotly contested constitutional issue in the era of the Roberts Court—the scope of First Amendment rights for people who want to contribute money to political campaigns—and the judges of the DC Circuit span a wide ideological range. Yet the opinion in the case, *Wagner v. Federal Election Commission*, was unanimous, representing the votes of all ten other active judges. (Garland and his colleagues heard the case under a federal law that assigns decisions on constitutional challenges to federal campaign-finance laws to the full court, rather than to the usual three-judge panel.)

They were likely unanimous because the decision is narrow. It pertains only to bans on "campaign contributions by individual contractors to candidates, parties, or traditional PACs that make contributions to candidates and parties." It exemplifies the work of a judge who is moderate by conviction, while making clear that being moderate does not mean stinting on upholding essential democratic safeguards, like those against threats to good government.

As an element of its narrowness, Garland's opinion squarely applied the law laid down in the Supreme Court's landmark ruling in *Citizens United*. Addressing only the problem of the literal kind of pay-for-play corruption, "a direct exchange of an official act for money," which is obviously so wrong that you might think few would be foolish enough to try it, the opinion showed why the contribution ban is still amply justified.

In striking ways, Garland's opinion resembles those that helped make Louis D. Brandeis an esteemed justice a century ago. At unusual length, it presents the background of the law, from its "historical pedigree" in the 1870s through the continuous substantial basis for it: in 1939, for example, a congressman called the campaign contributions in question "political immorality and skullduggery that should not be tolerated." In its deference to legislative history and to Congress, the opinion is also a model of judicial restraint.

Garland's opinion in the *Wagner* case showed what a fine choice he was for a Supreme Court split 4–4 between conservatives and liberals. (Here I may reflect a bias, because I have known him for many years.) President Obama picked him in the hope that his moderation would bring enough Republicans around to help confirm him as a justice. But from Obama's comments about Garland, at the University of Chicago and elsewhere, it seemed that after he announced the nomination, the president discovered even deeper reasons to feel buoyant about the choice.

On the Questionnaire for Judicial Nominees that Garland submitted to the Senate Judiciary Committee, one question asked him to list and provide capsule summaries of his ten most significant judicial opinions out of the more than three hundred that he had written. Each is a gem of concision and demonstrates an old-fashioned fidelity to analytical clarity and public service. The squib of the *Wagner* case is this: "Government contractors brought suit to challenge a provision of the Federal Election Campaign Act that barred individuals or firms negotiating or performing federal contracts from making federal campaign contributions. The unanimous en banc court of appeals upheld the constitutionality of the statute over First Amendment and Equal Protection challenges."

"The fight over the Garland nomination has been incredibly destructive to the public view of the Court," Evans Witt has said, "because it has reinforced the sense that the Court is a partisan institution." But Garland's capsule summaries were devoid of politics and solely about the law. They reflected the careful work of an outstanding judge in his twentieth year on the DC Circuit and, if the Senate eventually fulfills its duty under the Constitution and considers his nomination, the Supreme Court's next junior justice.

The Court is a political institution in three important senses: it often makes decisions that settle vital American disagreements about policies and values; it is a product of electoral politics and generally has no say about who becomes a member; and in the long period beginning almost half a century ago, justices appointed by Republicans have generally dominated it to a degree that most Americans do not realize, including many Republicans.

But it remains a legal institution, eager to convince the American public that that is what it is above all. It would be useful for the Court to have a ninth justice now who has distinguished himself by working hard to act on that view, even though, inevitably, he has shown the influence of his prior experience. It would be useful to have a new justice who recognizes, as President Obama wrote, that "today's constitutional arguments can't be separated from politics," yet who has the capacity to help the Court make persuasive decisions about those arguments—decisions that are not just political, because they are also worthy of respect as law.

A p p e n d i x

Biographies of Current Justices of the Supreme Court

All biographies are derived from the US Supreme Court website: https://www.supremecourt.gov/about/biographies .aspx.

Chief Justice

John G. Roberts Jr., chief justice of the United States, was born in Buffalo, New York, January 27, 1955. He married Jane Marie Sullivan in 1996 and they have two children— Josephine and Jack. He received an AB from Harvard College in 1976 and a JD from Harvard Law School in 1979. He served as a law clerk for Judge Henry J. Friendly of the US Court of Appeals for the Second Circuit from 1979 to 1980 and as a law clerk for then-associate justice William H. Rehnquist of the Supreme Court of the United States during the 1980 term. He was special assistant to the attorney general, US Department of Justice from 1981 to 1982, associate counsel to President Ronald Reagan, White House Counsel's Office from 1982 to 1986, and principal deputy solicitor general, US Department of Justice from 1989 to 1993. From 1986 to 1989 and 1993 to 2003, he practiced law in Washington, DC. He was appointed to the US Court of Appeals for the District of Columbia Circuit in 2003. President George W. Bush nominated him as chief justice of the United States, and he took his seat September 29, 2005.

Associate Justices

All justices are listed in descending order of seniority.

Anthony M. Kennedy was born in Sacramento, California, July 23, 1936. He married Mary Davis and has three children. He received his BA from Stanford University and the London School of Economics and his LLB from Harvard Law School. He was in private practice in San Francisco, California, from 1961 to 1963, as well as in Sacramento, California, from 1963 to 1975. From 1965 to 1988, he was a professor of constitutional law at the McGeorge School of Law, University of the Pacific. He has served in numerous positions during his career, including as a member of the California Army National Guard in 1961, the board of the Federal Judicial Center from 1987 to 1988, and two committees of the Judicial Conference of the United States: the Advisory Panel on Financial Disclosure Reports and Judicial Activities, subsequently renamed the Advisory Committee on Codes of Conduct, from 1979 to 1987, and the Committee on Pacific Territories from 1979 to 1990, which he chaired from 1982 to 1990. He was appointed to the US Court of Appeals for the Ninth Circuit in 1975. President Reagan nominated him as an associate justice of the Supreme Court, and he took his seat February 18, 1988.

Appendix

Clarence Thomas was born in the Pin Point community near Savannah, Georgia on June 23, 1948. He attended Conception Seminary from 1967 to 1968 and received an AB cum laude from Holy Cross College in 1971 and a JD from Yale Law School in 1974. He was admitted to law practice in Missouri in 1974 and served as an assistant attorney general of Missouri from 1974 to 1977, an attorney with the Monsanto Company from 1977 to 1979, and legislative assistant to Senator John Danforth from 1979 to 1981. From 1981 to 1982, he served as assistant secretary for civil rights, US Department of Education, and as chairman of the US Equal Employment Opportunity Commission from 1982 to 1990. From 1990 to 1991, he served as a judge on the US Court of Appeals for the District of Columbia Circuit. President George H. W. Bush nominated him as an associate justice of the Supreme Court, and he took his seat October 23, 1991. He married Virginia Lamp on May 30, 1987 and has one child, Jamal Adeen, by a previous marriage.

Ruth Bader Ginsburg was born in Brooklyn, New York, March 15, 1933. She married Martin D. Ginsburg in 1954 and has a daughter, Jane, and a son, James. She received her BA from Cornell University, attended Harvard Law School, and received her LLB from Columbia Law School. She served as a law clerk to the Honorable Edmund L. Palmieri, judge of the US District Court for the Southern District of New York, from 1959 to 1961. From 1961 to 1963, she was a research associate and then associate director of the Columbia Law School Project on International

Procedure. She was a professor of law at Rutgers University School of Law from 1963 to 1972 and Columbia Law School from 1972 to 1980 and a fellow at the Center for Advanced Study in the Behavioral Sciences in Stanford, California, from 1977 to 1978. In 1971, she was instrumental in launching the Women's Rights Project of the American Civil Liberties Union and served as the ACLU's general counsel from 1973 to 1980 and on the National Board of Directors from 1974 to 1980. She was appointed a judge of the US Court of Appeals for the District of Columbia Circuit in 1980. President Clinton nominated her as an associate justice of the Supreme Court, and she took her seat August 10, 1993.

Stephen G. Breyer was born in San Francisco, California, August 15, 1938. He married Joanna Hare in 1967 and has three children—Chloe, Nell, and Michael. He received an AB from Stanford University; a BA from Magdalen College, Oxford; and an LLB from Harvard Law School. He served as a law clerk to Justice Arthur Goldberg of the Supreme Court of the United States during the 1964 term; as a special assistant to the assistant US attorney general for antitrust, 1965–67: as an assistant special prosecutor of the Watergate Special Prosecution Force, 1973; as special counsel of the US Senate Judiciary Committee, 1974–75; and as chief counsel of the committee, 1979–80. He was an assistant professor, professor of law, and lecturer at Harvard Law School, 1967–94; a professor at the Harvard University Kennedy School of Government, 1977–80; and a visiting professor at the College of Law, Sydney, Australia, and at the University of Rome. From 1980 to 1990, he served as a Judge of the United States Court of Appeals for the First Circuit, and as its chief judge, 1990–94. He also served as a member of the Judicial Conference of the United States, 1990–94, and of the US Sentencing Commission, 1985–89. President Clinton nominated him as an associate justice of the Supreme Court, and he took his seat August 3, 1994.

Samuel Anthony Alito Jr. was born in Trenton, New Jersey, April 1, 1950. He married Martha-Ann Bomgardner in 1985 and has two children—Philip and Laura. He served as a law clerk for Leonard I. Garth of the US Court of Appeals for the Third Circuit from 1976 to 1977. He was assistant US attorney, District of New Jersey, 1977–81; assistant to the solicitor general, US Department of Justice, 1981–85; deputy assistant attorney general, US Department of Justice, 1985–87; and US attorney, District of New Jersey, 1987–90. He was appointed to the US Court of Appeals for the Third Circuit in 1990. President George W. Bush nominated him as an associate justice of the Supreme Court, and he took his seat January 31, 2006.

Sonia Sotomayor was born in Bronx, New York, on June 25, 1954. She earned a BA in 1976 from Princeton University, graduating summa cum laude and receiving the university's highest academic honor. In 1979, she earned a JD from Yale Law School, where she served as an editor of the *Yale Law Journal*. She served as assistant district attorney in the New York County District

Attorney's Office from 1979 to 1984. She then litigated international commercial matters in New York City at Pavia & Harcourt, where she served as an associate and then partner from 1984 to 1992. In 1991, President George H. W. Bush nominated her to the US District Court, Southern District of New York, and she served in that role from 1992 to 1998. She served as a judge on the US Court of Appeals for the Second Circuit from 1998 to 2009. President Barack Obama nominated her as an associate justice of the Supreme Court on May 26, 2009, and she assumed this role August 8, 2009.

Elena Kagan was born in New York, New York, on April 28, 1960. She received an AB from Princeton in 1981, an M Phil from Oxford in 1983, and a JD from Harvard Law School in 1986. She clerked for Judge Abner Mikva of the US Court of Appeals for the DC Circuit from 1986 to 1987 and for Justice Thurgood Marshall of the US Supreme Court during the 1987 term. After briefly practicing law at a Washington, DC, law firm, she became a law professor, first at the University of Chicago Law School and later at Harvard Law School. She also served for four years in the Clinton administration as associate counsel to the president and then as deputy assistant to the president for domestic policy. Between 2003 and 2009, she served as the dean of Harvard Law School. In 2009, President Obama nominated her as the solicitor general of the United States. A year later, the president nominated her as an associate justice of the Supreme Court on May 10, 2010. She took her seat on August 7, 2010.

Appendix

Retired Justices

All justices are listed in order of retirement.

Sandra Day O'Connor, (retired) associate justice, was born in El Paso, Texas, March 26, 1930. She married John Jay O'Connor III in 1952 and has three sons—Scott, Brian, and Jay. She received her BA and LLB from Stanford University. She served as deputy county attorney of San Mateo County, California, from 1952 to 1953 and as a civilian attorney for Quartermaster Market Center, Frankfurt, Germany, from 1954 to 1957. From 1958 to 1960, she practiced law in Maryvale, Arizona, and served as assistant attorney general of Arizona from 1965 to 1969. She was appointed to the Arizona State Senate in 1969 and was subsequently reelected to two two-year terms. In 1975, she was elected judge of the Maricopa County Superior Court and served until 1979, when she was appointed to the Arizona Court of Appeals. President Reagan nominated her as an associate justice of the Supreme Court, and she took her seat September 25, 1981. Justice O'Connor retired from the Supreme Court on January 31, 2006.

David H. Souter, (retired) associate justice, was born in Melrose, Massachusetts, September 17, 1939. He graduated from Harvard College, from which he received his AB. After two years as a Rhodes Scholar at Magdalen College, Oxford, he received an AB in jurisprudence from Oxford University and an MA in 1989. After receiving an LLB from Harvard Law School, he was an associate at Orr and Reno in Concord, New Hampshire, from 1966 to 1968, when he became an assistant attorney general of New Hampshire.

In 1971, he became deputy attorney general and, in 1976, attorney general of New Hampshire. In 1978, he was named an associate justice of the Superior Court of New Hampshire and was appointed to the Supreme Court of New Hampshire as an associate justice in 1983. He became a judge of the US Court of Appeals for the First Circuit on May 25, 1990. President George H. W. Bush nominated him as an associate justice of the Supreme Court, and he took his seat October 9, 1990. Justice Souter retired from the Supreme Court on June 29, 2009.

John Paul Stevens, (retired) associate justice, was born in Chicago, Illinois, April 20, 1920. He married Maryan Mulholland (deceased) and has four children—John Joseph, Kathryn, Elizabeth Jane, and Susan Roberta. He received an AB from the University of Chicago and a JD from Northwestern University School of Law. He served in the US Navy from 1942 to 1945 and was a law clerk to Justice Wiley Rutledge of the Supreme Court of the United States during the 1947 term. He was admitted to law practice in Illinois in 1949. He was associate counsel to the Subcommittee on the Study of Monopoly Power of the Judiciary Committee of the US House of Representatives, 1951–52, and a member of the attorney general's National Committee to Study Antitrust Law, 1953–55. He was second vice-president of the Chicago Bar Association in 1970. From 1970 to 1975, he served as a judge of the US Court of Appeals for the Seventh Circuit. President Ford nominated him as an associate justice of the Supreme Court, and he took his seat December 19, 1975. Justice Stevens retired from the Supreme Court on June 29, 2010.

Acknowledgments

I am especially grateful to Larry Kramer, the president of the Hewlett Foundation, and to the Foundation for a grant to Yale Law School that supported my research and travel for this book.

At the University of Pennsylvania Press, Damon Linker has been a fine editor—astute, efficient, and both encouraging and firm in ways an author working at journalism's pace requires. Gavriella Fried, Gigi Lamm, Laura Waldron, and their colleagues in marketing and publicity have been as dedicated, helping the book find readers and vice versa. My appreciation also goes to the Press's faculty board for approving my proposal for this book.

At the Supreme Court, the Public Information Office was welcoming and helpful, as the staff there is to every reporter who covers the Court. In particular, I thank Kathleen L. Arberg, the public information officer, and Patricia McCabe Estrada, the deputy public information officer.

At the law firm of Wiggin & Dana, Kim Rinehart, Tadgh A. J. Dooley, and others in its Appellate and Complex Legal Issues group write excellent and timely summaries of Supreme Court decisions. These were a great help to me especially in this project. (They were entertaining, too: "Greetings, Court fans! . . . und willkommen zurück! Oktober Term 2015 kicks off today with argument in OBB Personenverkehr AG v. Sachs (13-1067), a case which explores the contours of the commercial-activity exception to the Foreign Sovereign Immunities Act and is an early frontrunner for the title of 'most fun caption to say out loud.'")

To my former colleagues at the *New York Times* editorial board, I am grateful for the opportunity I had there to write about the Supreme Court for the editorial page and for other parts of the opinion section and, in particular, for the chance to learn and write about the death penalty.

I thank Nicholas Thompson, the editor of *The New Yorker*'s website, and Carla Blumencranz, its news editor, for their enthusiasm in publishing my work the past few years and for their superb editing.

Likewise, I thank Robert Wilson, the editor of *The American Scholar*; John Rosenberg, the editor of *Harvard Magazine*, and Jean Martin, a senior editor there; and Bob Kuttner, the coeditor of *The American Prospect*, for their excellent editing and for publishing my work.

Ninety-five percent of this book is fresh material. Selected passages of it appeared first on *The New Yorker*'s website and in *The American Scholar*, *Harvard Magazine*, and the *Missouri Law Review*. I am grateful to each of these publications for permission to use this material.

To everyone involved in creating and publishing *Legal Affairs* magazine as well—on the business and editorial staff, in the freelance diaspora, and at Yale Law School, Winterhouse Studio, Point Five Design, Lane Press, Tyler

Cooper & Alcorn, and elsewhere—my continuing appreciation and admiration.

The same for the students I have been fortunate to work with and learn from at Yale College and Yale Law School as a writing teacher. I am especially grateful to Emily Bazelon, with whom it has been a great pleasure to teach.

In the past few years, I have been fortunate to be a senior research scholar at Yale Law School and, when I have taught or cotaught there, a visiting lecturer in law. I am grateful to Dean Robert Post, Deputy Dean Al Klevorick, and others at the Law School who have been welcoming and helpful to me: in the dean's office, Beth Barnes and Georganne Rogers; in administration, Mike Thompson, Tangela Reid, Kevin Rose, and my assistant, Jennifer Marshall; in finance, Joe Crosby and Sue McDonald; in development, Tara Fitzpatrick; in information technology services, Susan Monsen, Gerard Armoogam, Steven Verrastro, and John Zito; and in the library, Blair Kauffman, Julian Aiken, Fred Shapiro, John Healy, Evelyn Ma, and Sarah Ryan. It would have been impossible to write this book without the great resources of the Yale Law School Library and without the support of its world-class team.

Garrett Epps, the consulting editor for the American Justice series of which this book is part, set a high standard in writing the first volume, *American Justice 2014: Nine Clashing Visions on the Supreme Court.* All of us with the privilege of writing a successor volume will measure our book against Garrett's. As the *Atlantic's* Supreme Court correspondent, in addition to serving as a professor of law at the University of Baltimore School of Law, he reports and comments on the Court with uncommon excellence.

Acknowledgments

I want to thank some friends who have provided inspiring examples through their splendid work as journalists, writers, lawyers, public servants, problem-solvers, scholars, teachers, and more: Todd Crawford, Deborah Fallows, James Fallows, Krista Fogleman, Jamie Gorelick, Chuck Harris, Ira Helfand, Michael Ignatieff, David Ignatius, Vicki Jackson, Lew Kaden, Jeffrey Leeds, Susan Liss, Robb Moss, Steve Pearlstein, Lee Rainie, Jay Reich, Paulette Rosen, Rafe Sagalyn, Patti Saris, Richard Schottenfeld, Arthur Segel, Ellen Semonoff, David Skeel, Doug Smith, Bob Taylor, Ana Vollmar, Michael Vollmar, Richard Waldhorn, and Bill Yeomans.

Rob Shapiro is also on that list, and I dedicate this book to him: for a friendship lasting fifty-two years and counting, for weekly phone calls in thirty-six of those years while we have lived in different places, and for the model he provides of learning as if he will live forever and living as if every day matters.

My immeasurable thanks to my family, as always, for their love and support: my sisters, Joanna Caplan and Margi Caplan; my brothers-in-law, Bob Blaemire and Philip Bricker; Nick, Ana, Dan, Nora, and Adam; and especially my wife, Susan, and our daughter, Molly. While our daughter-in-law Emily came into the family too recently to have had a role in this writing adventure, it is a pleasure to have her join us.

CPSIA information can be obtained at www.ICGtesting.com
Printed in the USA
BVOW08*2237160916

462401BV00001B/1/P